The Beatitudes

Living Life According To Jesus' Instruction

Pastor Jerry Helton

The Beatitudes

Copyright 2016 by Jerry W. Helton

Published by The House of Prayer Church via
CreateSpace

Transcribed by: Carol McKechnie and Joyce
Stewart

Edited by: Carol McKechnie, Bill Honaker and
Craig Shreiner

Cover design by Craig Shreiner

Unless other wise indicated, Bible quotations are
taken from the King James Version of the Holy
Bible.

CONTENTS

	Preface	1
1	Blessed Are The Poor In Spirit	5
2	Blessed Are They That Mourn	21
3	Blessed Are The Meek	35
4	Blessed Are They That Hunger And Thirst After Righteousness	49
5	Blessed Are The Merciful	59
6	Blessed Are The Pure In Heart	71
7	Blessed Are The Peacemakers	87
8	Blessed Are The Persecuted	99
9	Conclusion	111

PREFACE

This book was conceived, created, and completed in secret as a loving gift for our beloved pastor, Jerry Helton. Imagine with me Pastor Jerry's words if he had been aware of what we have been up to these past few months...

"There ain't nothing this Georgia mountain boy, who loves soup beans and chocolate cake and fried chicken, could ever say that is worthy of printing except for the truths of God's Word!"

And that is exactly what you have in your hands... God's banquet-size truths, sprinkled with Pastor Jerry's humor, heart, and realness. The Beatitudes from Jesus' Sermon on the Mount will unfold in a powerful way on these pages. Each chapter is taken from one of a nine-part sermon series devoted to this challenging and life-changing text.

For over 30 years of ministry, our "Georgia mountain boy" pastor has taught himself before teaching the Body of Christ. He has been known to say that there are times the Word of God steps on his toes. Sometimes it gets all over his shins.

And at other times, Jesus gets right in his face! We may not get to see this toe stepping or shin bruising but one thing we do see is that it always finds a way to his heart.

We are a blessed people to see our pastor not only teach God's Word but also live it out in front of us.

Pastor Jerry gave his life to the Lord as a nine year old boy on June 4, 1959. His heart was changed and is still changing. He has learned love from a God who is love.

"And may the Master pour on the love so it fills your lives and splashes over on everyone around you."
1 Thessalonians 3:12 (The Message)

Our Pastor Jerry, through Jesus, keeps each of us soaking wet!

In this book, he introduces the Beatitudes to us as radical and revolutionary in today's culture. This is how it happened:

"And seeing the multitudes, he went up into a mountain:
and when he was set, his disciples came unto him:
And he opened his mouth, and taught them, saying,

Blessed are the poor in spirit: for theirs is the kingdom of heaven.
Blessed are they that mourn: for they shall be comforted.
Blessed are the meek: for they shall inherit the earth.
Blessed are they which do hunger and thirst after righteousness: for they shall be filled.
Blessed are the merciful: for they shall obtain mercy.
Blessed are the pure in heart: for they shall see God.
Blessed are the peacemakers: for they shall be called the children of God.
Blessed are they which are persecuted for righteousness' sake: for theirs is the kingdom of heaven."
Matthew 5:1-10

Blessed assurance! As you see, with every "Blessed," there is an incredible promise from a God who cannot break His promises.

This mountain message is a prescription for life – for a peace that cannot be taken and a joy that cannot be stifled. This message is just for you and it comes from God who loves and delights in you.

You have been given a "springboard" into God's living water. Because of His great love for you He is beckoning you to jump in.

If you are already in the deep, you will never settle for dry again. If you are in the shallows, quit wading, and come into a deeper, gushing relationship with a God who refreshes and sustains.

And if you haven't jumped in yet – what are you waiting for? The water is PERFECT!

Janice Saylors
October 2016

BLESSED ARE THE POOR IN SPIRIT

FOR THEIRS IS THE KINGDOM OF HEAVEN
Matthew 5:3

For many people, if not for most people, happiness is based upon all the circumstances in their lives being right...having all their ducks in a row. I've heard it put this way: They are part of the "when and then" thinking. When I get the right job, then everything will be all right. When I find the right mate, then I'll be happy. When I have kids, then I'll be happy. Or, when the kids get out of the house, then I'll be happy. They are always waiting on the "when" to be right before they can be happy. We fall into thinking that outward circumstances are what make us happy.

Jesus, in God's word, cuts directly counter to all that thinking. As a matter of fact, it is right the opposite. Jesus insists that happiness and contentment are not based on outward circumstances at all but depend on an attitude within.

When we read in Matthew 5, we come across Jesus giving an attitude check.

In this Scripture, Jesus says when we have the right way of thinking, then happiness, contentment, and joy can follow. It follows right attitude. In fact, this section of Scripture is known as the Be-Attitudes. Be in the right attitude.

Someone once said the only way to change another person's attitude was either by deep psychotherapy, a deep religious experience, or brain surgery. I tend to agree with the second one. I know that when we come into a dynamic encounter with the living Lord Jesus Christ, when He comes into our heart and saves us, He changes everything.

As a matter of fact, 2 Corinthians 5:17 tells us *"old things are passed away, behold all things are become new."*

So I am convinced that a personal encounter with Jesus Christ can change even the worst attitude as the Holy Spirit of God works in us and through us to make us more like His Son, Jesus Christ.

"And seeing the multitudes, Jesus went up into a mountain and, when He was set, His disciples came to him."

It is interesting that as Jesus looked out on the crowd, and as He looks out at our House of Prayer Congregation, He sees all of us. But He sees us individually also. When He sees us, He doesn't just see the outward, He knows us. Jesus knows where we are. He knows our greatest needs. He knows our fears – maybe ones we haven't even expressed. He knows our failures. He knows our heart's desires. And He still loves us! He knows everything about us and He loves us. And Jesus, looking out on the crowd, saw them just as He sees us. He saw the crowds; but He knew the needs.

"Looking out and seeing the multitudes, He sat down." A Jewish Rabbi, when he was ready to teach, would always sit. When he sat down, this would be the cue for everybody around that now was the time to teach them.

"And He opened His mouth and taught them saying, Blessed are the poor in spirit: for theirs is the kingdom of heaven. Blessed are they that mourn: for they shall be comforted. Blessed are the meek: for they shall inherit the earth. Blessed are they which do hunger and thirst after righteousness: for they shall be filled. Blessed are the merciful: for they shall obtain mercy."

The word blessed is sometimes translated as happy, or oh, how happy, or happy many times over. The original word in Greek is an emphatic word so it is not just happy, but man! Really happy! So verse seven says "Happy are the merciful for they shall obtain mercy."

"Blessed are the pure in heart: for they shall see God. Blessed are the peacemakers: for they shall be called the children of God. Blessed are they which are persecuted for righteousness' sake: for theirs is the kingdom of heaven. Blessed are ye when men shall revile you, and persecute you, and shall say all manner of evil against you falsely, for my sake. Rejoice and be exceeding glad: for great is your reward in heaven: for so persecuted they the prophets which were before you." Matthew 5:2-12

There was a time in House of Prayer history that many of us memorized this section of Scripture. Would you agree that Jesus does everything perfectly? I believe that. I believe when Jesus does something, He does it exactly the way He intended to do it. I don't think He ever had to say "Oops. I messed up there." That's pretty common at Jerry Helton's house but I don't believe it was with Jesus. I believe Jesus does everything right.

Chapters 5-6-7 are known as the Sermon on the Mount and comprise the longest recorded teaching of Jesus that we have in the New Testament. So it is completely by design and is no coincidence that He begins teaching with these words *"Blessed"*...Happy...Really Happy..."*are the poor in spirit.*"

We will find as we continue to study these Be-Attitudes that the rest of them build off of this first one, just like building on a foundation of these right attitudes that are so critical. If you are not poor in spirit, it will become very difficult, if not impossible, to find the contentment and happiness that God wants to be ours.

The Amplified Bible puts it this way: *"Blessed, happy, to be envied, and spiritually prosperous are the poor in spirit."* It then defines spiritually prosperous as "being with life-joy and satisfaction in God's favor and salvation regardless of outward conditions." Wow!

When I read this, it just gripped me. I said "Lord, am I satisfied with Your favor and salvation regardless of my outward conditions? Regardless of what's going on around me? Regardless of the chaos? Regardless of the personal things? Regardless of the family things? Regardless of the societal things? Am I finding my satisfaction in Your favor and in Your salvation?"

"Blessed" -- happy, to be envied, to be spiritually prosperous, that is with life-joy and satisfaction with God's favor and salvation regardless of outward conditions – *"are the poor in spirit:"* Then the Amplified goes into the poor in spirit and says they are the "humble, rating themselves insignificant" – *"for theirs is the kingdom of heaven."*

So what does this mean? What was Jesus saying when He said the poor in spirit? Those who rank themselves insignificant? Surely He wasn't talking about possessions. The verse doesn't say blessed in spirit are those who are poor. Jesus doesn't condemn having possessions anywhere that I can find. But He warns us solemnly and over again about not allowing possessions to own us. So He's not talking about possessions.

And it does not say Blessed are the self-debased or those who think they are worthless, nothing, nobody. I love that saying "God doesn't make bad investments." He has invested in you through His Son, Jesus Christ. You are special to Him. Every one of us is special to Him. He saw the multitudes but He sees each individual. He sees us right now.

Poor in spirit is the humble realization that we are totally unable to save ourselves. That we are totally dependent on God's grace and God's mercy in our lives. Jesus lived that out. He walked out what this true humility looks like.

In Philippians 2:8 it says when He was living as a man Jesus *"humbled Himself and was fully obedient to God."* Even when that caused His death on the cross. He humbled Himself. He emptied Himself of all He could have demanded as God.

The rich in spirit know it all. They can answer all the questions. The poor in spirit realize their deficiencies and limitations. The rich in spirit are self-sufficient; the poor in spirit are Christ-dependent.

This reminds me of a story in Luke 18 that relates an encounter with Jesus by what it describes as a rich, young ruler. This young man came to Jesus asking, *"Good Master, what shall I do to inherit eternal life?"* Jesus says, *"Why do you call Me good?"* Jesus knew full well what was in the young man's heart. He knew this was a self-made, self-sufficient guy. So Jesus says to him, *"You know the commandments – do not commit adultery, do not kill, do not steal, do not bear false witness, honor your Father and Mother."* And the young ruler says, *"Man, I've done all these."*

Max Lucado in his book <u>Applause from Heaven</u>, gives his account of this encounter in Luke 18. He says, "How Jesus keeps from laughing is beyond me. The question that was intended to show the rich young ruler how he falls short, only convinces him that he stands tall." I love this. He says, "He is a child dripping water on the floor while telling his Mom he hasn't been out in the rain."

None of us can tell God how good we are. This guy was basically saying "Tell me how to invest, tell me what it's going to cost me, because I want to inherit eternal life. Whatever it is, I'll do it." He didn't need a system. He needed a Savior. He didn't need to rewrite his resume; he needed a Redeemer. If you're looking for a system, or if you're looking to be good enough, you'll never get there. And Jesus looked at this guy and He says something that He tells no one else in all of Scripture. He tells this young man one thing: *"Go sell all you have and give it to the poor and come follow me."* Why do you think he told that to this man and no one else?

In our lives there is going to be some thing or some one that is going to dominate the top position. God says He needs to be that Some One.

Scripture is very clear that if a man gains the whole world and loses his own soul, what does it profit him?" God knows that, for us to be happy, for us to find that contentment, that joy, and all that He wants to provide for us, that will only come as we realize and totally become dependent upon Him and let Him become ruler of our lives.

But there are a lot of others that want to be King of the Hill or King of the Mountain in our life. Careers ... too many. I've been there, seen that. Athletics can be addictive when that adrenaline gets pumping. You always want to see how far you can go, what you can do, how much can you teach, how much can you show others.

When I was coaching I saw too many guys and gals who sacrificed the most productive years of their lives.

They sacrificed years they would never have again with their kids trying to climb that ladder to succeed in their careers. They think they will pour their lives into their company and, boy, the company is going to see that and see how invaluable and indispensable they are.

It is that "when and then" thing. When I get there, then I will have time for everything else. Only when they get to that point and realize they have sacrificed all this to the company, they find they are just a number on the payroll. And the company says, "We appreciate all you've done but we're having to downsize and, well, we're sorry but we have to let you go."

So Jesus says to this young man, "You want to know how to get eternal life? Just follow me. Put Me at the top of your life. Everything else is second."

Scripture says the young man left sorrowful. It grieved him. Jesus knew that apart from Him, we are nothing.

One of the most dangerous places any person can ever get is thinking they are just a little bit good. To think, Jesus can't do without me. Or to think, Jesus owes me. I go to House of Prayer church all the time; I do stuff for them all the time. Jesus must appreciate all I do for Him.

Poor in Spirit means humbling ourselves and understanding our total dependence upon Him. Ephesians 2:8-9 are very familiar verses that state it clearly: "*For by grace are you saved through faith and that not of yourselves, it is the gift of God: not of works, lest any man should boast.*" It's grace. It's mercy.

And then the blessings that come from being poor in spirit, what are they? Jesus says of the poor in spirit, *"theirs is the kingdom of Heaven."* What's the Kingdom of Heaven? The Kingdom of Heaven that Jesus is referring to is not the place we go when we die if we're Christians. That's just Heaven. But the Kingdom of Heaven is far more.

The Kingdom of Heaven is the sphere or the realm over which Jesus rules. That's why He could say the Kingdom of Heaven is now here among you. It is walking with Him as Lord.

And what kind of life is it when we quit trying to be our own ruler and relax and trust Him and follow Him? It's a life that brings grace. James 4:6 says, *"But He giveth more grace."* That is why the Scripture says: *"God opposes the proud but gives grace to the humble."* One of the first acrostics I remember learning is this: Grace is **G**od's **R**iches **a**t **C**hrist's **E**xpense.

This is so true! The realization that I deserve nothing, and yet Jesus looks down and sees me and loves me and He pays the tab. He picks up the bill for my sin, for my failures, for my shame. And Scripture says God takes this and, as a bookkeeping transaction, He imputes Jesus' righteousness to my ledger. He puts it on my account.

So now when God looks at the ledger for those of us who have accepted Jesus as our Savior, God sees only the righteousness of His Son. And in that righteousness, He sees all the riches, all the inheritance.

Can you imagine what it would be like to be the son of the richest man in the world and have a good relationship with him? We are sons and daughters of the King of the Universe! The Creator God! And the relationship He has with you and with me is His desire for us to know Him as He knows us. And it delights Him to give us the kingdom. It is a life that brings grace.

The second benefit of being poor in spirit is it reduces my stress. Stress can kill you; have you heard that? Things build up. When I'm humble, poor in spirit, I don't have to know all the answers. It is so refreshing sometimes. It is refreshing to know that I can resign as General Manager of the Universe. God doesn't expect me to have it all together and under control.

God doesn't expect me to be perfect. He knew I wasn't. He knew I couldn't be. That's why Jesus died for me. But when He looks at me, He sees the "perfectness" of His Son. That's grace! When I realize that I'm not perfect, I can relax because I don't have to expect perfection from those around me. Now that is freeing.

In Philippians 4:12-13 New Century Version, Paul puts it this way: *"I know how to live when I'm poor, and I know how to live when I have plenty. I've learned the secret of being happy at any time in everything that happens; when I have enough to eat and when I go hungry; when I have more than I need and when I do not have enough. I can do all things through Christ because He gives me strength."*

We are all familiar with this 13th verse and recite it often. But the context of it is Paul's realization that, through Christ, he can be poor in spirit and can be totally dependent upon Christ.

Paul is saying we can learn this contentment, this trust, this right attitude because Christ is doing that in our lives. When stress is reduced in my life, happiness can increase. You want to get rid of some stress? Start thinking like Jesus thought. Develop this poor in spirit attitude.

One more thing in addition to bringing a life of grace and reducing my stress, being poor in spirit also improves my relationships with other people. Let me share this powerful quote from a cancer survivor, someone who has lived expecting death at any time, whom God has amazingly and miraculously strengthened and raised back up.

"If you have a relationship with God, and if you have the right attitude, you will learn to ask the one question in life that covers everything: How can I help you? What can I do for you?"

It's not about me. It's about me serving you. Those who have been forgiven should be forgiving people.

Don't fall into the trap of having been forgiven much by God and failing to extend that forgiveness to others.

Paul is a great example of someone who was poor in spirit and learned this secret. His life modeled grace. Talk about someone who could have been stressed out! But he was relaxed in Jesus and was forgiving. Paul is quite a contrast to the rich, young ruler in Luke 18. The rich, young ruler made a name for himself in his world and yet we never read about him in Scripture anymore.

Paul was an up-and-coming young Pharisee. He was trained as part of the religious elite, the ruling body of Judaism and he was persecuting these renegades; and then one day on the way to Damascus he encountered the living Lord and it changed his life forever.

The group that he'd been such a part of, the group that had looked up to him is now looking *for* him. He has to be slipped out of town in a basket because they are going to kill him! Now God changes his name from Saul to Paul and we know him as the Evangelist Missionary. He got a new name and a new life.

I loved when my son said to me one day, "Dad, I'm not the same person." You know what? Neither am I. And neither are you when you meet Jesus. Old things are passed away. All things are new.

Blessed are the poor in spirit; for theirs is the kingdom of Heaven.

BLESSED ARE THEY THAT MOURN

FOR THEY SHALL BE COMFORTED
Matthew 5:4

In verse four of Jesus' sermon, we come to *"Blessed are they that mourn: for they shall be comforted."* One of the first things that speaks to me as I look at this is a section of Scripture from Isaiah 61. This is a mission statement of the coming Messiah and what He would accomplish. It is this very scroll that would be handed to Jesus in the Synagogue on the Sabbath – after His baptism and His sojourn in the wilderness where He fasted for 40 days and nights and then suffered temptation by Satan. He turns to this section of the scroll and reads.

It really speaks to my spirit whenever I read this, to think that Jesus read these very same words that I am reading! He probably read them in Hebrew, but these are the words He read that morning as Luke tells us.

It says, *"The Spirit of the Lord God is upon me; because the Lord hath anointed me to preach good tidings unto the meek;*

He hath sent me to bind up the broken hearted; to proclaim liberty to the captives, and the opening of the prison to them that are bound; to proclaim the acceptable year of the Lord, and the day of vengeance of our God; to comfort all that mourn; To appoint unto them that mourn in Zion, to give unto them beauty for ashes, the oil of joy for mourning, the garment of praise for the spirit of heaviness..." (Verses 1-3)

I want you to notice the exchange. Look at what we are giving up and at what God is giving to us through the ministry of Jesus Christ and the Holy Spirit. He's giving us beauty for ashes. He's giving us oil of joy for mourning. He's giving us a garment of praise for the spirit of heaviness. *"...that they might be called trees of righteousness, the planting of the Lord, that He might be glorified."*

After He read this Scripture that Sabbath morning, Luke 4:21 tells us Jesus said to those who were listening, *"This day is this Scripture fulfilled in your ears."* Basically He is saying, "That's My mission statement; now let's get on with it."

So I glean from this that part of His mission or reason for coming is to comfort those that mourn.

It would be a little while later when Jesus would gather His followers together on a mountainside near the Sea of Galilee and say *"Blessed are they that mourn: for they shall be comforted."* The men wondered and discussed among themselves, seeking to know what He was talking about. What did He mean by that?

The word that is translated here as mourn is a very intense word, used most often in Scripture to describe the intense grieving or sorrowing when someone very close, such as a family member or very close friend, has died. In the book of John chapter 11 we have the story of Martha and Mary and their brother Lazarus who gets very sick and dies.

They had sent for Jesus to come. You remember the story, that Jesus delayed His coming, not so Lazarus would die but so God would be glorified. So when Jesus and His disciples arrive, Lazarus is in the grave, the friends of Mary and Martha are there grieving, sorrowing and mourning with them.

Martha and Mary each come to him saying, *"If only you'd been here, my brother would not have died."* (Verse 21)

Jesus gives us this promise that we as believers have amplified over the years and in our lives. In verses 25 and 26 Jesus said to them, *"I am the resurrection and the life: he that believeth in Me, though he were dead, yet shall he live; And whosoever liveth and believeth in Me shall never die. Believest thou this?"* As He asked them this question, He confronted them where their faith met their emotions. Their emotions were grieving and sorrowing over the loss of their brother; they were raw. But He said, "Listen to Me! If you can believe it, I am the resurrection and the life. The person who puts their faith and trust in Me is never going to die."

That was a hard saying. Their brother was lying in the grave ... what did Jesus mean he would never die? As the story plays out we understand more and more the comfort He is talking about here. Remember right after He spoke these words to Mary and Martha, He looks around and verse 35 – shortest verse in Scripture yet one of the most profound and powerful – says *"Jesus wept."*

When the Jewish friends of Mary and Martha see Jesus weeping, their comment is "Look how much Jesus must have loved Lazarus!"

Indeed, Scripture tells us to weep with those who weep; rejoice with those who rejoice. I believe not only was Jesus weeping in sadness for them, but I think He was saddened by looking around and seeing the hopelessness of death without Him. We know the rest of the story: how Jesus speaks and Lazarus comes back to life.

As a pastor with over 30 years of ministering, often times at the funeral or death of a family member or a friend, many times I have preached from this passage of John that the comfort we have as believers, for the Christian who dies, it is not the end at all but the transition of life into eternity; it is walking *through the valley of the shadow of death*, as the Psalmist said, because death is gone. Jesus has been victorious over death!

So for the family of a loved one who has died as a believer who trusts in the Lord, we have this comfort that death is not the end, that not only will we see them again in Heaven with the Lord, but we will BE with them. We will be around the throne not only with them but with our Savior Jesus Christ forever!

There is tremendous comfort in that. The Lord says when we grieve, when we mourn, there is comfort.

Paul is talking about the same thing in the book of 1st Thessalonians. This letter is to the first century Christians in Thessalonica – after Jesus has been killed, buried, resurrected and ascended into Heaven with the angels telling the gawking on-lookers "He's coming back!" Early Christians and all Christians since that day have been looking for His return. It is a promise. He hasn't returned yet, but He will come back!

So the Thessalonians were looking and some were worried because their parents and grandparents had died and Jesus hadn't come yet. They were confused and uncertain. So in chapter four, verse 13 the writer says, *"But I would not have you to be ignorant, brethren, concerning them which are asleep, that ye sorrow not, even as others which have no hope."* Be sure you get this verse and we'll refer to it later. Ignorant here means without knowledge, unknowing, not unintelligent or stupid.

It goes on: *"For if we believe that Jesus died and rose again, even so them also which sleep in Jesus will God bring with him. For this we say unto you by the word of the Lord, that we which are alive and remain unto the coming of the Lord shall not prevent them which are asleep."* (Verses 14-15)

He's speaking about the rapture of the church. When the Lord comes in the air and catches up the body of believers, He will bring with Him the Christians who have already died and have been with Him to meet the church in the air.

I believe we will meet with them and after that will usher in the period of the Great Tribulation. *"For the Lord Himself shall descend from heaven with a shout, with the voice of the archangel, and with the trump of God; and the dead in Christ shall rise first: Then we which are alive and remain shall be caught up together with them in the clouds, to meet the Lord in the air; and so shall we ever be with the Lord. Wherefore comfort one another with these words."* (Verses 16-18)

These words and the words Jesus spoke have continued to be a tremendous comfort, a tremendous promise; we do not just *hope* for but *know* because it is sure in the word of God for those who have died in the Lord.

This is great comfort only if they were a believer in the Lord Jesus Christ. And only if *you* are a believer in the Lord Jesus Christ. If that loved one has died without accepting the Lord Jesus Christ and His grace and forgiveness, then there is an eternity separated from the God Who loves them. We need to know that God loves us so much.

Our dear friend, Edwin Messerschmidt who has gone to be with the Lord, was a missionary and a servant of the Lord for many years. He shares that the first time he ever heard the gospel was when he was a teenager in Minnesota. The preacher was preaching on John 3:16, that God loved the world so much that He gave His Son Jesus Christ to die on the cross for the sins of the world. Edwin says he had never heard this before. What gripped him was that a Person he never knew would love him so much He would die for Edwin's sin. Edwin thought if He would die in my place so I can live eternally with Him, this is a Man I want to get to know. If He loves me this much that He would give His life for me, surely I can give the rest of my life to serve Him. That was the motivation behind Edwin coming to faith.

I can tell you that for me it was quite different. I grew up in church where at nine years old I heard a message at a week-long Revival that was one of judgment that those who die without the Lord Jesus will be in hell, separated from God for eternity.

At that age I wasn't running a drug cartel, I wasn't trafficking in prostitution, I hadn't murdered anyone. But I knew that sin was not doing what God told me to do and if I didn't accept Jesus Christ, I would spend eternity separated from Him.

That service I was so under conviction I was afraid I would die that night without being saved. I knew that if I died without being saved, I would go to hell. So my prayer that night was, "Jesus, if You let me live 'til tomorrow night, I'll get saved." God honored that prayer. I have no idea what the message was that night. All I knew was I had made God a promise; He had spared me, and I knew there was eternal life, there was forgiveness for my sin, there was a Jesus Who loved me waiting for me right there. I couldn't wait for that invitation. So for me it was that realization that there is a heaven to gain, and there is an eternal separation from God in hell for those who don't know Him.

Often when we talk of the comfort of God, which is so powerful for families coping with loss through death, that is our Hope. Referring back to 1st Thessalonians 4:13, it says, *"We sorrow not as those who have no hope."* If you die without the Lord Jesus Christ in your heart, if you die before you make a commitment to serve Him, you will spend eternity separated from Him. That's the word of God.

Know this: It is not God's will that anyone should go to hell. He did not create hell for all the bad people to go to. God loved us so much He gave His Son Jesus to die so all the bad people could see the righteousness of Christ and be saved.

That's His desire! That's His will for every person. We need to receive Him; we need to trust Him; we need to accept Him.

There is tremendous comfort for those who mourn at the loss of a loved one when they've been saved. There's that promise. But I believe looking at verse four, there is another part of this that's connected, that builds upon verse three about the poor in spirit.

Poor in spirit refers to our lost-ness, that we need a Savior, that causes me to cry out *"Woe is me. I am undone,"* just as Scripture says. Now at nine years old I didn't go home, smite my breast and say "Woe is me; I am undone!" All I knew was I needed Jesus to let me live until the next night so I could get saved. I didn't want to die and go to hell. That was a mourning and grieving in my spirit because I had seen my lost-ness. I had seen the desperate plight I was in. I knew that I had sinned and if I died without Jesus, I would go to hell.

There is this mourning for our sinfulness that prepares our hearts to repent and accept Him. Second Corinthians 7:10 in the New Living Translation says it this way: *"The kind of sorrow God wants us to experience..."*

Wait a minute. You mean God wants us to sorrow? Sorrowing, grieving, mourning – that's a part of life, folks, whether you are saved or lost. It continues: *"...leads us away from sin and results in salvation. There's no regret for that kind of sorrow. But worldly sorrow, which lacks repentance, results in spiritual death."*

There can be a difference between legitimate mourning and false inappropriate mourning. Remember David, when his son Absalom was killed, was distraught saying *"Absalom, Absalom! Would to God that I had died instead of you!"* David's general, Joab, comes to him and basically gives him a Gibb's slap up the back of the head reminding David that his entire army had fought for him. They needed his appreciation for saving him, not his despair that it required taking his son's life.

There is a part of mourning that can result in self-pity and there is a worldly sorrow that lacks repentance and is more a "sorry I was caught," "sorry I was found out," "sorry there are consequences I must face," but there is no true repentance, no mourning of the heart. There is no conviction, no crying out, "I am a sinner in need of a Savior." That results in spiritual death that will doom your soul to hell.

There is a parallel passage in Luke 6:20-22 that says this. *"And Jesus lifted his eyes on his disciples, and said, Blessed be ye poor: for yours is the kingdom of God. Blessed are ye that hunger now: for ye shall be filled. Blessed are ye that weep now: for ye shall laugh."*

Let me tell you the rest of my story. I have heard people say that when they accepted Jesus it was like a weight lifted off their shoulders. I can understand that. It is the weight of those sins, of that guilt. They are now free from the burden. They have the comfort of forgiveness, of peace, of the blood of Jesus Christ creating and making us a new person.

What I remember of that night is, I remember laughing. Laughter has always been a big part of my life but I remember laughing that night because I felt so good. I don't know if it was because God spared me and I didn't go to hell, or if it was because I knew that now Jesus was my Savior and I would spend eternity with Him.

But Luke is saying when we weep, especially for our sinfulness, Jesus is ready to turn that weeping into laughter. Into freedom. Into joy.

Have you mourned? Have you realized your need of a Savior? If so, you understand the comfort that comes from knowing Him. He gives comfort for the mourning.

Blessed are they that mourn; for they shall be comforted.

BLESSED ARE THE MEEK

FOR THEY SHALL INHERIT THE EARTH
Matthew 5:5

The atheist, Friedrich Nietzsche, is noted for the statement "God is dead." Nietzsche in one of his writings wrote this: "Assert yourself. Care for nothing except yourself. The only vice is weakness and the only virtue is strength. Be strong. Be a superman. The world is yours if you work hard enough for it." Another young man read Nietzsche's writings and was very impressed by him and sought to become that superman. His name was Adolph Hitler. He was very much influenced by the writings of this atheist and we know how that ended.

I don't know how much Jesus spoke of strength, but I know Jesus spoke of meekness quite often. As He began His sermon that day on the mountain overlooking the Sea of Galilee and the valley there, the third Beatitude in Matthew 5:5 is *"Blessed are the meek: for they shall inherit the earth."*

I want you to look with me at lessons to be learned about meekness.

The first thing to realize is that meekness is not weakness! The best definition I have heard for meekness is "power under control." A good example of that is in Matthew 11, verse 29 where Jesus says *"Take my yoke upon you and learn of Me; for I am meek and lowly in heart; and ye shall find rest unto your souls."* Jesus claimed meekness.

There came a day that Jesus saw what was going on with the changers of money and the selling of sacrificial animals and all the commerce that was going on in the Temple; and as He sat there and watched, He began braiding strips of leather together and when he was finished, He turned over the tables of the money changers and used the whip to drive the men out of the Temple saying, "My House is supposed to be called a House of Prayer and you are making it a shopping mall. Get out of here!" That's the Jerry Helton translation, of course.

On that day, Jesus didn't look weak, but He did exhibit "power under control." That control, I believe, was from His Father and from the Holy Spirit.

So one of the things this says to me clearly is that I need to allow God, God's word, and the Holy Spirit of God to guide me, to direct me, to teach me as I do this thing called Life. It's as though you were getting in your car and saying, "OK, Jesus, I'm behind the wheel and I'll drive, but I need You to tell me where to go. If You say go straight or turn right or turn left or go back, that's what I'll do. Because I want You to guide me, I want You to control my life, my journey through this life, and my destination."

I want to share some of the things I have learned about meekness. Referring to 11:29 again, He says *"Take My yoke upon you and learn of Me."* Meekness to me is teachable. *"Learn of Me."* He wants us to know Him.

The best way to do that is in His word. Learn how Jesus reacted to different situations. Remember several years back when they came out with the wrist bands and mugs and many things that said WWJD? I like that. What would Jesus do? That was a reminder that we need to be teachable. How did Jesus handle His accusers? How did Jesus handle those who rejected Him? How did He handle those who would make Him King?

To those who are involved in athletics, the word is coachable. What a shame it is to have a young athlete that has been gifted with athletic abilities, that has so much potential, but is not coachable. That will drive you crazy. That can get you fired. I know a number of coaches faced with this situation who think "If I could take that kid's ability and put it in the body of this kid who is coachable, we'd be unstoppable. What a waste!"

One of the things I have learned about meekness is that it means allowing God to be in control. It means humility. It means not having to be in control, not stubborn, not arrogant, to be more and more like Jesus. We need to learn of Him.

Another thing I've learned about meekness is that it means gentleness. The Message translation of Romans 14:1 really pops to me. *"Welcome with open arms fellow believers who don't see things the way you do. And don't jump all over them every time they do or say something you don't agree with – even when it seems that they are strong on opinions but weak in the faith department. Remember they have their own history to deal with. Treat them gently."* Accepting people. Loving people. Treating them with respect and gentleness.

Galatians 6:1 says this: *"Brethren, if a man be overtaken in a fault, ye which are spiritual restore such a one in the spirit of meekness; considering thyself lest thou also be tempted."* How do we respond when someone we love or are close to or work with messes up big time? Do we say "I tried to tell you! You wouldn't listen! That was a stupid thing to do!" Meekness is gentleness, not judgmental. I'm learning that.

Another thing meekness is teaching me is that meekness is submitting to the Holy Spirit of God and allowing Him to control my life. Here's a shocker: If you live, you are going to be hurt. To live and love, you are going to be hurt more deeply. People you love and care for are going to do things that hurt you more deeply. Most of the time they aren't even aware they have hurt you; if it was intentional, it would hurt even more.

How we as Christians react, respond, and handle those hurts can teach us much about how we are doing at being meek. When we are hurt, there is a knee-jerk reaction of going to a defensive mode.

Do we react by retaliating, getting even, or with forgiveness, love, kindness? Meekness is allowing God to be in control.

You've heard the expression of someone flying off the handle. If you've ever had an axe head fly off the handle, you know what that means. It's dangerous! If you've ever flown off the handle, you know you were not in control. That happens. It's not pretty. People can be hurt. If we allow people to "push our buttons" and make us react or respond, they are basically controlling us right then.

In First Corinthians 13:4-7, the New Living Translation says it this way: *"Love is patient and kind. Love is not jealous or boastful or proud or rude. It does not demand its own way. It is not irritable and it keeps no record of being wronged. It does not rejoice about injustice but rejoices whenever the truth wins out. Love never gives up, never loses faith, is always hopeful, and endures through every circumstance."*

Love is choosing to allow the Holy Spirit to work through me so I do not react to those buttons being pushed or to circumstances. Meekness is allowing Him to be in control.

Another thing I've learned is that meekness is more about being more understanding and less demanding.

Philippians 2:3-5 in The Message says *"Don't push your way to the front; don't sweet-talk your way to the top. Put yourself aside, and help others get ahead. Don't be obsessed with getting your own advantage. Forget yourselves long enough to lend a helping hand. Think of yourselves the way Christ Jesus thought of Himself."* When things aren't going the way I want them to go, am I demanding or am I understanding? Do I take out my frustrations on those around me? You know ... kick the dog, snarl at my wife and kids? Or do I allow those circumstances to be a learning lesson for me?

What happens when you pray for patience? It seems God puts you in a circumstance that allows you to learn greater patience...when you didn't want to *learn* patience, you wanted to *have* patience. God lets the trying of your faith produce patience in you. As you learn patience, one of the lessons God is teaching me, is that meekness can also be learned.

Notice in this passage from Philippians, there are three things we are told *not* to do. Don't push yourselves to the front; don't sweet-talk your way to the top; don't be obsessed with getting your own way.

Then there are three things we are told to do. Put yourself aside so you can help others, forget yourself and lend a helping hand, think of yourself as Christ Jesus thought of Himself. In this Philippian passage Jesus talks about taking on Himself the form of a servant and humbling Himself, becoming obedient even unto death on the cross.

So the writer is helping us see that meekness is more understanding and less demanding of our own way. We have a choice. We can choose to be rude or crude or we can choose to be patient and kind. We can choose to be helpful or we can choose to be a pain in the neck. We can choose to be demanding or we can choose to be understanding. We can choose to let the Holy Spirit take over.

As a believer, the Spirit lives within us and desires to do just that.   The more we practice that and learn to do that, the more clearly we are able to hear His voice and obey Him.

Lastly, meekness is learning to disagree agreeably. Here's another shocker: You can't please everyone all the time. If you've been trying to do that, just relax.

I read about a preacher who went to a seminar and one of the break-out sessions was titled "How to Please 100% of the People."

He walked into the session and it was packed, standing room only. So the speaker got up and said, "Well, about 50% of the people are going to be happy when you come and 50% will be happy when you leave." And that was it.

For me, a good indicator of my spiritual maturity, how I'm doing in my meekness, is how I interact with, or how I get along with, the disagreeable. Meekness does not mean compromising my convictions. That's not what I'm talking about. But it is handling conflict with gentleness.

A few years ago we were going through a little book in our staff devotions and one of the sections was "Pick the hills that are worth dying on." In other words, choose the battles we are willing to fight for. Not everything has to be life or death.

Seven years into our marriage, God blessed Barbie and me with our first child. She was a blessing. She was blue eyed, blond headed, fair skinned, and by the time she was in kindergarten, she was Daddy's precious little angel.

We were blessed to have one of the best kindergarten teachers there ever was. Miss Janice Cochran was a godly woman and a super teacher.

She had olive complexion and dark hair, and she wore bright red lipstick. It looked good on Miss Cochran; but the first time I saw my five-year-old daughter with red lipstick daubed on her mouth, I about lost it. I thought she was headed for a life of sin, I thought, "Save her, Jesus!" I panicked!

Barbie had to calm me down, reminding me that Paige's teacher wore bright red lipstick and she said, "I can see you're not going to be able to handle the girl thing. But if you can just trust me, I will guide our little daughter through girlhood. You just try to relax and breathe."

And it worked! So that was a hill I didn't need to die on, a battle I didn't need to fight for. This is true, not just with our kids, but with other members of our Christian family.

Here at House of Prayer our motto says "In essentials, unity; in non-essentials, liberty; but in all things, love." I heard that over and over growing up at House of Prayer.

We need to get along with others even when we disagree. It has been good for me to understand that God has designed His church this way.

First Corinthians 12:4-7 in The New Living Translation says, *"There are different kinds of spiritual gifts, but the same Spirit is the source of them all. There are different kinds of service, but we serve the same Lord. God works in different ways, but it is the same God who does the work in all of us. A spiritual gift is given to each of us so we can help each other."* Notice that. We aren't given spiritual gifts so we can brag about ourselves, but so we can build up, edify, the body of Christ.

God has placed us here to serve Him and to serve one another. We're not all the same; we're not supposed to be! Someone asked me recently about the elders of our church. We have a former Baptist pastor; we have a couple of former Methodist pastors; we have one who comes from an Assembly of God background; we have one who comes from more of a charismatic background; and we have one who comes from a heathen background. All of these men love God, and love you, and love each other. God creates us differently; He gifts us differently for His glory. We are not supposed to be the same.

Verse 17 and 18 in the same chapter says. *"If the whole body were an eye, how would you hear? Or if your whole body were an ear, how would you smell anything? But our bodies have many parts, and God has put each part just where He wants it."*

That is so true physically, of course, but is applied to us spiritually as well. God places us within the body of Christ to serve Him with our different gifts. One of the things I love, that has been so beneficial to me growing up in the House of Prayer, is the differences. We were founded in the 1950s as an Interdenominational Church. Now I'll tell you a secret. When I filled out my application for college my freshman year, the form asked for my denomination. I put Baptist because that was easier to spell. The second year I put Methodist, figuring since it was a Methodist school maybe that would get me a scholarship. It didn't. My third year of college, I wrote out Interdenominational. I thought they'd be so impressed that I could spell that, they'd give me my bachelor's degree right away! They didn't.

The body of believers who founded the House of Prayer came from so many different backgrounds – Baptists of several kinds, Methodists of several kinds, Assemblies of God, Church of God, and others. God just put all of them, and He puts all of us, together worshipping Him. Sometimes when people ask me what denomination we are, I love to say "generic." They wonder how we can get along, how a church can function, how we can minister to the community, to the youth, with mission trips, etc., when we have so many different beliefs.

I love when someone asks that because I can answer, "Because we have the same Savior. Because we have the same Lord. Because we have the same heavenly Father, and we have learned over the years to focus on that thing that is essential on which we agree: Jesus Christ." When we get to Heaven, we want to see Jesus. We want to see the gates of pearl, the street of gold, the river of life, we want the grand tour.

A story relates that St. Peter will say, "First you have to take this class called Heaven 100." In this class, God will take us in and straighten out all of our theologies. We may be pleasantly surprised and we may be astonished, but all of us taking that class will have gotten to it through the blood of Jesus Christ. We will not have worked our way there; we will not have earned our way there. We are there because of Jesus and what He has done for us. Part of being meek is being able to agree to disagree and keep Jesus central in all things.

The rest of that verse says *"...for they shall inherit the earth."* While I have been focusing on the lessons I have learned about meekness, I have been asking God what the second part means.

There was a Christian comedian who attended Baylor University years ago. Baylor is a Baptist school in Texas. This guy played football for Baylor and was a lineman. His first game, he was lined up right across from an All American, and he was thinking "I've got to really let him know I'm here as soon as the ball is snapped. If I don't, he'll be pushing me around the whole game."

So the ball was snapped. When he came to, his face mask and his face were buried in the sod. As he was digging the turf out of his mask and spitting grass out of his mouth, the All American stood over him and said, "The meek shall inherit the earth."

I know that is not what God means. First century Jewish understanding of inheritance is that they considered the land promised to Abraham, Isaac, and Jacob to be the fulfillment of God's promise. As I look at this, I believe the promise of God is that all He has and is will belong to us. It is our inheritance.

Blessed are the meek; for they shall inherit the earth.

BLESSED ARE THEY THAT HUNGER AND THIRST AFTER RIGHTEOUSNESS

FOR THEY SHALL BE FILLED
Matthew 5:6

Craig Shreiner, at his ordination service, left us with this charge: Stay thirsty for the things that matter. Matthew Patrick at his Youth Sunday presentation admonished us to "long for God." In fact, he went on to say if we long for anything else in life more than we long for God, we are missing the mark.

I think that is what the Psalmist in the very familiar Psalm 42 refers to when he says *"As the deer longs for the streams of water so I long for you, Oh God. I thirst for God the Living God."* (NLT) And then in Psalm 63 he says *"Oh God, you are my God. I earnestly search for you. My soul thirsts for you, my whole body longs for you in this parched and weary land where there is no water."* (NLT)

When I memorized The Beatitudes as a young teenager, I assumed it to be linear. For instance, if you weren't poor in spirit, perhaps you were merciful; if not merciful, perhaps a peacemaker. I saw it as an either/or situation and tried to see where I could fit into that. As I look more and more into this Scripture, I begin to see a building process.

Those of you who remember a Coach named John Wooden will remember that he coached at UCLA, running a string of national titles in the NCAA. He was a masterful teacher as well as coach and he developed what he called a "Pyramid of Success." Every block of achievement was built on top of what had gone before.

As I look at the way Jesus laid this message out, I realize He builds His message in much the same way, using building blocks. I believe hungering and thirsting for God begins when we realize that we are poor in spirit, that we are totally bankrupt, that we cannot save ourselves, that we are in need of a Savior, that we can't do enough good things or get righteous enough to merit God's favor.

Seeing that we are poor in spirit -- the first Beatitude --, brings us to the second one that we cry out, we mourn and grieve in our desperation, where we long and yearn for a

Savior, for a rescuer, for a deliverer. Then there is a progression to the third where we yield or submit to His sovereignty where we meekly say, "Lord, I need you! I'm desperate for you!" So these first three Beatitudes are essential to bring us to the place in the fourth where He says *"Blessed are they that hunger and thirst after righteousness: for they will be filled."*

This brings up two questions: What does a healthy spiritual life look like? And What are the results of a healthy spiritual life?

What does it mean to hunger and thirst after righteousness? I've read that some scholars say in the original language hunger and thirst implies a hungering for the whole thing. In other words, those who hunger and thirst are not just looking for a little finger sandwich or an hors d'oeuvre plate. They don't want a little sandwich; they want the whole loaf of bread. They don't want a sip of water; they want the whole glass. It is a thirsting, a craving, a desire for Him and His righteousness. This craving is a hunger for more and more of God.

I have shared with you how I accepted Christ as a young boy. Not long after that, I said to my Dad, "I wish I could be saved again." I was missing that emotion, that exhilaration, that newness of fellowship."

So I ask myself now: Am I craving God more now than I did ten years ago? Am I more thirsty for Him than I was 20 years ago? By the grace of God and patience of a congregation, I have pastored House of Prayer for more than 33 years. So my question to myself is, "Am I longing for God more today than I was as a young man 33 years ago?" Jesus says "Blessed are they who hunger and thirst after God."

Thinking about this, my thoughts went to Moses and how he hungered and thirsted after God. I spoke earlier of Moses and meekness. Scripture describes Moses as one of the meekest men who ever lived. Remember that meekness is not weakness! Moses saw an Egyptian mistreating a Hebrew slave, and he rose up and took the Egyptian out! Moses stood boldly before Pharaoh, leader of the strongest nation on earth with the strongest army at that time. And yet, when Moses was out tending the sheep and saw the burning bush, he encountered God and fell on his face before the Most High removing his shoes to honor the holy ground on which he stood.

Moses witnesses God's mighty power bringing the powerful nation of Egypt to its knees to the point that Pharaoh would tell Moses to "Take these Hebrews and get out of here!"

We see Moses at the Red Sea with the Egyptian army in hot pursuit and God telling Moses to hold up his rod, and the waters parted for millions of Hebrews to cross as on dry ground. And then the Sea closed and destroyed the army of Egypt. We see Moses eating manna that God provided every day except on the Sabbath. We see Moses drinking the water flowing from the rock. Moses had seen God at work! It amazes me that in Exodus 33, verse 18, Moses begs of God, "...show me Your glory." What? Hadn't he seen God's glory in the plagues, the water from a rock, the parting of the Sea? What was he thinking? But know this: Moses had an insatiable appetite for *more*. He hungered and thirsted and longed for God. Do you? I'm convinced that Moses knew all these things he saw God do was just scratching the surface.

I am so blessed. I can sit in my pew and look on the choir, or stand in the pulpit and look out at the congregation and, because of you allowing me into your lives in different ways over the years, I know a little bit of His story in you. His glory. The victories. The struggles. The hurts. The times that you have been desperately in need and God has been there. I see God's glory in all of you. I see His righteousness and His power.

We need to not lose sight of that ... but we need to never be satisfied because we are only scratching the surface! There is so much more. Jesus is saying, "Blessed are you who have seen your Spiritual bankruptcy, have grieved and mourned over it, who have submitted and yielded to me, who have thirsted and longed and craved and hungered for me for there is a filling with which you can be filled."

Someone said the key to willpower is want-power. People who want something badly enough usually can find a way to achieve it. I read an illustration of a student approaching his spiritual leader asking "Master, how can I truly find God?" The master replied, "Walk with me to the river." They walked to and into the middle of the river. The student looks around and the master puts his hand on the student's head and pushes his head under the water. The student is still for a minute but then begins to try to raise up and the master's hand is heavier and heavier on his head. Soon the student is flailing and struggling and is fighting desperately to get up out of the water. The master removes his hand and the student comes up gasping for breath. The master said, "When you long for God as much as you longed for air, you'll find Him." Am I longing for Him as much as I long for the air I breathe or the food I eat?

I understand hungering and thirsting, but asked God "What's this righteousness?" In Matthew 5, verse 10, Jesus says *"Blessed are those who are persecuted for righteousness' sake: for theirs is the kingdom of Heaven."* There is that word again. And in verse 11, *"Blessed are ye when men shall revile you, and persecute you, and shall say all manner of evil against you falsely, for My sake."* I think Jesus is saying righteousness is Himself; we hunger and thirst for Him, His righteousness, His glory.

The reason Christians were being persecuted, and are being persecuted today by ISIS and other demonic forces around the world, is because of Christ. You can belong to the garden club, the rock society, you can belong to anything in the world, and all is cool. But when you belong to Jesus and proclaim that, there is a target on your back from the enemy. I would rather be in a fight belonging to Him with a target on my back than to be left at ease by the world and wake up in Hell. Jesus says, "Blessed are you who hunger and thirst for Me."

At the heart of most major religions of the world is usually a person. With Buddhism it is Buddha. With Islam it is Mohammed. With Hinduism it is Krishna. With Christianity it is Jesus. But at that point the comparison ends completely.

If you ask the followers of Islam how they find salvation in their religion, they will point you to the Quran. If you ask the same of a Buddhist, look at the noble truths Buddha wrote, they will instruct you. Jesus Christ did not come just to teach truths. He taught truth but He said, "*I* am *the truth*." Jesus Christ pointed the way to God, but He said "*I* am *the way*." "*No man cometh unto the Father but by Me*." (John 14:6) He and He alone is the Way, Truth, and Life. Jesus was saying, When you hunger and thirst for Him, you shall be filled!

Christianity is not just a way of living. It is first and foremost a relationship with the person of Jesus Christ. The condition of a healthy spiritual life is a hungering and thirsting for God. The result is that we are filled, satisfied. The original language for "shall be filled" is a passive tense. It is not something we can do for ourselves. God does it for us. Our responsibility is not to pursue satisfaction, but to pursue the Savior. Our responsibility is to seek Him. The result of a healthy spiritual life is contentment that only God can provide.

I want to compare a couple of different people that illustrate appropriately what this verse says. The first is a famous Hollywood actress, Raquel Welch.

These are her words: "I'd acquired everything I wanted yet I was totally miserable. I thought it peculiar that I had obtained everything I wanted since I was a child ... I had wealth, fame, a wonderful career, beautiful children, a lifestyle that seemed terrific ... yet I was totally, miserably unhappy. I found it frightening that one could acquire all these things and be so miserable." The lies of the world are that we should seek after these things and, when we find them, we'll be happy. Many people abandon God, abandon the faith of the fathers, to try to find that place that was supposed to bring satisfaction only to find it was a lie, a mirage. There is nothing there but emptiness. And Jesus tell us, If you really want filled, if you really want satisfied, if you want that hungering and thirsting and craving quenched, come to Me.

You may not know this second person. His name is Nicholas Herman. Nicholas was a short order cook and dish washer. He got to thinking about his life and realized he was on a nowhere road, going nowhere. He believed in God, believed in Jesus, but hadn't gotten to the point of questioning whether he was really saved. One day he was watching the trees blowing in a coming storm, and he realized the reason that tree could withstand the storm was because of something down deep that was unseen.

What he couldn't see gave stability to what he could see and keeps it from toppling over in the storm. That day he decided to make his life an experiment. It was what he called a "habitual silent secret conversation of the soul with God." Soon those around him sensed an awesome contentment and peace that was amazing. After his death, they found several of his writings, some of his conversations, even some of his prayers which they compiled and put in a book called <u>Practicing the Presence of God.</u> You know him as Brother Lawrence.

A Hollywood star who had everything the world said would make her happy and her resulting emptiness. A monk who didn't even own his own clothes and his resulting fullness. He lived such a life that his friends collected his writings and put them in a book. He had learned the secret that God is with us every day. So every day he went about communicating with Him as though He were there with him.

Blessed are those who hunger and thirst after righteousness: for they shall be filled.

BLESSED ARE THE MERCIFUL

FOR THEY SHALL OBTAIN MERCY
Matthew 5:7

You will remember the incident that happened at the Cincinnati zoo where the little boy managed to climb a fence and get into the gorilla pit. For ten agonizing minutes, people watched (and photographed!) the gorilla dragging the little boy around. Now a gorilla would be capable of crushing a child's skull with very little effort, so there was certainly real cause for panic. It was decided to put the animal down to save the little boy. I firmly believe that God has appointed us stewards over His creation and that includes animals; but when we heard of the petition with hundreds of signatures and saw signs that said the parents should be punished because the gorilla's life matters, I was astonished. Jack Hannah, the wild animal expert, proclaimed that the child would not have survived if they had not put the gorilla down.

It seems that these days everyone's life matters except Christians and innocent babies.

Christians around the world are facing martyrdom. Hundreds of Christians around the world are seeing their children killed before their eyes because of their faith in the Lord Jesus Christ. We hear little – if anything – about this on the news. Franklin Graham tweeted that, at the time this incident was taking place at the zoo, about 120,000 innocent babies were aborted in this country. There is no outcry. We are living in a mixed-up society.

Because we live in this mixed-up time, if we aren't careful, it becomes easy for us to become skeptical or even merciless. With that in mind, we consider this fifth Beatitude: *"Blessed are the merciful: for they shall obtain mercy."*

The first four Beatitudes clearly address our relationship with our Heavenly Father – recognizing that we are poor in spirit, grieving over our lost condition, humbly seeking Him, and hungering and thirsting for Him. The next four address our relationships with one another. This reminds me of the Ten Commandments.

As you look at the commandments God gave Moses that have become the basis of our laws, the first four are about our relationship vertically -- with God -- and the next six are about our relationships horizontally -- with others.

God's Commandments and Jesus' Beatitudes are both saying in not such a subtle way, when you get everything right with God, when your life is in line with Him, when you are at peace with Him ... THEN you are ready to work on your relationship with others.

Scripture calls us to be holy. Peter quoting Leviticus in his first letter says, "*Be ye holy for I am holy.*"(1 Peter 1:16) Luke records Jesus' message differently than Matthew: "*Be ye therefore merciful, as your Father also is merciful.*" (Luke 6:36) So we are to be both holy and merciful! What does it mean to be merciful?

Vine's Dictionary of New Testament Words describes it this way: "Mercy is the outward manifestation of pity. It assumes needs on the part of him who receives it and resources adequate to meet that need on the part of him who shows it." Arthur Pink says it this way: "Mercifulness is a holy compassion of soul whereby one is moved to pity and goes to the relief of another in misery. Being merciful is being moved to action by what we see and what we feel."

What does that look like? Here are three different ways:

First is showing mercy materially. James 2:14-17 says *"What does it profit, my brethren, if someone says he has faith but does not have works? Can faith save him? If a brother or sister is naked and destitute of daily food, and one of you says to them, 'Depart in peace, be warmed and filled,' but you do not give them the things which are needed for the body, what does it profit? Thus also Faith by itself, if it does not have works, is dead"* When you have the means to relieve a need, do nothing about it, but say "I'll pray for you," James is saying that amounts to nothing.

First John 3:17-18 puts it this way: *"But whoever has this world's goods, and sees his brother in need, and shuts up his heart from him, how does the love of God abide in him? My little children, let us not love in word or in tongue, but in deed and in truth."* (NKJV) Galatians 6:10 instructs further: *"Therefore, as we have opportunity, let us do good to all, especially to those who are of the household of faith."* (NKJV)

We have a ministry at House of Prayer called A Servant's Heart which seeks to identify skills and abilities of those in our congregation and match them up with needs of members. That's what mercy looks like in a material way.

Bear in mind Elijah's Closet, The Cottage Food Bank, and Benevolence Committee have been serving the practical way through food, clothing, money for prescriptions or other needs since House of Prayer was formed. When you do this, it is inevitable that you will be taken advantage of at some time or other. We know that. We try to be as wise as we can, as discerning as we can. We don't want to be enablers. At the same time, we are not going to let the fact that we might be taken advantage of by one or two along the way keep us from ministering to those multiple numbers who are needful. So we ask the Lord for wisdom and understanding and we will do our best to be wise stewards of that with which we are entrusted and we will leave it all up to Him.

There was a time that a group of folks went down to Homestead, Florida, to put a roof on the house of Russell and Kerry Black, missionaries we support. Neighbors and folks going by would comment about all these folks from Georgia working on their house, and by the way, how much are they charging?

When Russell told them that these folks had paid their own way down, were paying their own way to stay so they could be of help, people would say, "Who even does that? Who takes a week of vacation, spends their own money, to go work on someone's house?"

Well, God's people do that. The material part of mercy is observable to an unbelieving world.

Secondly is showing mercy in emotional ways. 2 Corinthians 1:3-5 says *"Blessed be the God and Father of our Lord Jesus Christ, the Father of mercies and God of all comfort, who comforts us in all our tribulation, that we may be able to comfort those who are in any trouble, with the comfort with which we ourselves are comforted by God. For as the sufferings of Christ abound in us, so our consolation also abounds through Christ."* (NKJV) This is what that says to me: There isn't one of us that has not at some time in life felt as though we were being put through the meat grinder. It might be physical things, relational things, hurting because someone you love is going through a hard time. But the Spirit of God has come along side of you, maybe in the form of a friend who comes over to just be with you, maybe in the form of a cake or a pie and that act of mercy and love has lifted your spirits, has raised your hope. You are reminded that someone not only knows what you are going through but also cares. This is the reason for this Scripture: The comfort God gives to us equips us to share that same kind of love, that same kind of compassion, that same kind of mercy to those around us when they go through tough times. This is what emotional mercy looks like.

There is another practical way to show the emotional side of mercy and that is with patience. God is saying to me that if I am going to be truly merciful, I will be more patient with those who are different. A very well-known pastor said, "I believe into every life a few weirdos must fall." First Thessalonians 5:14 in the NLT says, "*Brothers and sisters we urge you to warn those who are lazy. Encourage those who are timid. Take tender care of those who are weak. Be patient with everyone.*" I think he added that last part just for me! I spent many years as an educator working with special needs students. Because of that, I have a great deal of patience with those who are unique.

I will confess, my struggle is with those who are obnoxious. I don't mind being merciful to them but I want to do it at a distance. You know what I'm talking about here – those people who seem to leave a wake of hurt feelings, damaged egos, angry hearts everywhere they go.

If I can remember that people who hurt others are probably hurting themselves, it helps me to be less critical and a little less judgmental. It isn't easy, but it is needful. Be merciful. The emotional part of mercy is awesome.

Thirdly is showing mercy in spiritual ways. Colossians 3:13 says in The Living Bible, *"Be gentle and ready to forgive; never hold grudges. Remember, the Lord forgave you, so you must forgive others."*

Here's something about forgiveness. When we are the recipient, it feels so easy and so right. When we are to forgive, it feels so hard and so wrong. Have you ever had to ask someone's forgiveness? It's hard. And it is like a cool glass of water on a hot day to hear them say, "I forgive you." We need that. We want that. Why is it so hard for us to turn around and forgive? Do we want them to grovel and crawl and beg for our forgiveness? But the reason I can forgive others and the reason I *need* to forgive others is so I am following God's forgiveness to me.

Scripture tells me that if I fail to forgive others, He will fail to forgive me. We need to be forgiving one with another. Forgiveness is the most beautiful picture of spiritual mercy. When someone fails, when someone sins, when a brother or sister sins and it becomes public knowledge, do you rub it in or rub it out? Does it grieve your heart; do you empathize? Do you call them, stand up for them? Nothing is more beautiful than forgiveness, the spiritual part of mercy.

So the question is: How do I become more merciful? There are three steps listed in the familiar story in Luke 10:25-37. The Living Bible tells it this way: *"One day an expert in the Law of Moses came to test Jesus' orthodoxy by asking Him this question: 'Teacher, what does a man need to do to live forever in heaven? Jesus replied, 'What does Moses' law say about it?' 'It says,' he replied, 'that you must love the Lord your God with all your heart, and with all your soul, and with all your strength, and with all your mind. And you must love your neighbor just as much as you love yourself.' 'Right!' Jesus told him. 'Do this and you shall live.' The man wanted to justify his lack of love for some kinds of people, so he asked, 'Which neighbors?'"*

So Jesus replies with an illustration we know well about the Jewish man travelling from Jerusalem to Jericho who was attacked by robbers who beat him, stripped him, robbed him and left him for dead. By chance a Jewish priest came along, saw him, crossed to the other side of the road and passed him by. Then a Jewish temple assistant walked over, looked at him lying there but went on his way. Then a despised Samaritan came along and, when he saw the man, he felt pity. That's step one to answering God's call to be merciful: We need to see with God's eyes. How does God see people?

I'm convinced God sees people so much differently than we do. He sees them on the inside. We see one another on the outside – cleaned up, spiffed up – we don't see the wounds, hurts, heartaches in people.

When Barbie and I were ministering in San Francisco in the late 70s, things looked very weird on the outside. We learned to pray, "Lord, let me see with your eyes. Let me see into the heart. Let me see what's behind the weird clothes." It starts with seeing with God's eyes. When we see the news, what is God seeing? When we get reports from the mid-East, when missionaries come back from Africa or Haiti, we see the pictures. But what does God see?

The second step: The Samaritan felt deep pity. What does God feel? Hebrews 13:3 says, *"Remember them that are in bonds, as bound with them; and them which suffer adversity, as being yourselves also in the body."* The NLT says, *"Remember those in prison as if you were there yourself."* Your first thought might be "Well, they are there because they've done something wrong." Who of us has not done something wrong?

The third step: The Samaritan tended to the man's needs. You see, what this Samaritan saw and felt moved him to action. He put the injured man on his donkey and took him to the nearest inn. The Samaritan was most likely travelling on business, had things to do. Very seldom is being merciful a convenient thing. But he took the time to spend the night tending to this man's wounds and when he left in the morning he gave the innkeeper what The Living Bible refers to as two twenty-dollar bills. Obviously this Bible paraphrase was done some years ago! King James says two denarii which would be about a day's wage. These days it would take a good bit more than that. Today it would probably take about $200. He even offered to repay any more money the innkeeper might have to spend when he returned.

These three steps: God let me see with Your eyes; God let me feel what You feel even if I can only handle a little bit of it; and then, God let me put mercy into action in Jesus' love. Be ye merciful. There is something some people call a boomerang principle that says this: You'll be happy (that is, blessed) many times over when you show mercy to others because then mercy will be shown to you.

Have you tried that and it didn't work out that way? That can happen. Any time you love people, you are going to be wounded. Any time you practice mercy, you take the risk of running into people who will take advantage of you.

C.S. Lewis wrote this: "To love at all is to be vulnerable. Love anything and your heart will certainly be wrung and possibly broken. If you want to make sure of keeping it intact, you must give your heart to no one, not even to an animal. Wrap it carefully around with hobbies and little luxuries. Avoid all entanglements. Lock it up safe in a casket or coffin of your selfishness. But in that casket – safe, dark, motionless, airless – it will change. It will not be broken; it will become unbreakable, impenetrable, irredeemable, merciless."

Blessed are the merciful; for they shall obtain mercy.

BLESSED ARE THE PURE IN HEART

FOR THEY SHALL SEE GOD
Matthew 5:8

Someone has said our "attitudes" determine our "altitude" in our walk with the Lord. So it is in the sixth Beatitude: *"Blessed are the pure in heart, for they shall see God."* This is a call to purity. One of the definitions of the word "pure" is "to cleanse one's mind and one's emotion." Scholars say there are really two meanings to this word in this verse.

The first is "to make pure by cleansing from dirt or from filth or from contaminations" and it's used when we're talking about refining gold or silver. The second definition is "having no dual allegiance." To the ancient Greeks it meant "straightness, honesty or clarity."

Warren Wiersbee says about this verse: "The basic idea is integrity and singleness of heart."

In Matthew 6:24, Jesus will say later in this sermon: *"No man can serve two masters; for either he will hate the one and love the other, or else he will be loyal to the one and despise the other. You cannot serve God and mammon."* *(NKJV)* Always before when I'd read this verse, what would come to my mind would be Psalm 24:1-4 *"The earth is the Lord's, and the fullness thereof; the world, and they that dwell therein. For He hath founded it upon the seas, and established it upon the floods. Who shall ascend into the hill of the Lord? Or who shall stand in His holy place? He that hath clean hands, and a pure heart; who hath not lifted up his soul unto vanity, nor sworn deceitfully."*

As I thought about that, I got a title for this chapter: "Pure Inside and Outside." Clean hands and a pure heart. My grandmother, Miss May Kelley, was named "Mossy" by one of the grandkids and it stuck. Oftentimes Mossy would see someone and say, "They are pretty on the inside and out." She was referring to the fact that not only were they physically attractive or handsome but also their inner spirit was beautiful because of their love for the Lord and the humility that flowed from that. So in honor of Mossy May, the title of this chapter is: "Pure on the Inside and Out." Clean on the inside. Not just on the outside. Not just when people are watching.

There was an article in an old Daily Bread about a father and a son riding one day down a country road. They passed a watermelon patch just off the road. They could see the patch and the watermelons lying there. The vines had started dying so the melons were ripe. The daddy pulled off to the side of the road. The son said, "Daddy what're you going to do?" The daddy said, "I'm gonna get us one of those melons. You watch. You look out."

So the daddy slipped over into the patch and he had a big melon and he yelled back to his son, "Son, look. Be sure no one is coming. Look both ways." The little boy yelled back, "Daddy, shouldn't I look up, too?" We need to be careful about the lessons we are teaching our kids. We want to be clean on the inside as well as on the outside.

The Pharisees in Jesus' day were great at outward purity. They were the religious leaders who had expounded a list of DOs and DON'Ts. If you want to go to heaven, you must do this and don't do that. If you want to be pure, you do this and you don't do that. You don't do that, but you do this. The Pharisees thought that performing their religious acts religiously made them pure. But they were wrong.

Today there are still a lot of people around believing the same way the Pharisees thought. They think there are many religious things that they DO that will make them pure. Just like the Pharisees, they're wrong. It doesn't happen that way. We spend so much time on the outside, making the outside look good. It's the inside that God really focuses on.

In I Samuel 16, Samuel is coming to anoint one of Jesse's sons as king. He looks at Eliab and the others. Then in verse 7: *"But the Lord said unto Samuel, 'Look not on his countenance, or on the height of his stature; because I have refused him; for the Lord seeth not as man seeth; for man looketh on the outward appearance, but the Lord looketh on the heart'."* Proverbs 21:2 says: *"Every way of a man is right in his own eyes; but the Lord pondereth the hearts."*

That's why, when Jesus was laying the foundation for this message, He did not say, "Blessed are the pure, for they shall see God." Instead He says -- and it's very important -- *"Blessed are the pure IN HEART, for they shall see God."* It's not just the outward where others can see. It is that which is within. Where God looks. Here the heart refers to who we really are. It's like the command center inside each of us that controls and directs our thinking and our emotions and our will.

Scripture has a lot of references to this. The book of Psalms says we can see our reflection in water. So the heart reveals who we really are. Proverbs 4:23: *"Keep thy heart with all diligence; for out of it are the issues of life."* Jeremiah 17:9-10: *"The heart is deceitful above all things and desperately wicked; who can know it? I the Lord search the heart, I try the reins, even to give every man according to his ways, and according to the fruit of his doings."* Jeremiah understood that as we strive for a pure heart, the heart can be deceptive. And it can be deceptively wicked

One time Billy Graham was preaching about the sins we deal with and he said the sins of this world can be summed up with one main problem. Our basic problem isn't a race problem. It isn't an economic problem. It isn't a prosperity problem. Today we can even say the basic problem of the world is not a terrorism problem.

Billy Graham said our basic problem is a heart problem. The problem of sin is not that the world around us is so contaminated. It's that which is within us. We don't sin because of our surroundings. We sin because of what's in our heart. We need to come to terms with that. We need to understand what we're dealing with when Jesus says, *"Blessed are the pure in heart, for they shall see God."*

You may think, "But I'm not *all* bad." I ran across the Schopenhauer's Law of Entropy. I've never heard of this; but it says that if you put a spoonful of wine in a barrel full of sewage, you get sewage. If you put a spoonful of sewage in a barrel of wine, you still get sewage. Scriptures warn us of the danger of even a little sin kept tucked away in our hearts. We've become so comfortable. We've dealt with the big issues. I'm not a murderer. I'm not this. I'm not that. We just keep this little sin harbored and tucked away. We are warned over and over and over of the dangers. Jesus said, *"Blessed are the pure in heart, for they shall see God."*

How do I guard the purity of my heart? Scripture is plain in II Corinthians 5: 17: *"Therefore, if any man be in Christ, he is a new creature; old things are passed away; behold, all things are become new."* Ezekiel 36:26 says, *"A new heart also will I give you, and a new spirit will I put within you; and I will take away the stony heart out of your flesh, and I will give you an heart of flesh."* He is saying He will give us a heart that is sensitive, that can feel and respond to the spirit of God.

Often when I am praying for someone, I find myself praying, "Lord, keep them sensitive to Your Holy Spirit." We want to be able to hear Him. When God speaks, we need to know that it is God speaking.

One of the things that has helped me over the years about hearing the voice of God, I learned at a Gothard conference. It is so important when we hear God speaking to know it is God speaking. Now if you don't know it is God, Scripture is plain that we try the spirits until we know it is God. But once we know it is God telling us to do something or not do it, then we must obey quickly. The longer we delay, the more time and the more room that gives the enemy to convince us that it's not God. So we need to respond quickly once we know it's God.

When David had sinned and was confronted with his sin, he prays this prayer of repentance in Psalm 51:10. I pray that God would give a gift of repentance as we hear His word. David prays, *"Create in me a clean heart, O God; and renew a right spirit within me."*

Hebrews 12 lays out some thoughts on how to walk out this relationship with a pure heart before God. Hebrews 12 begins with a reference to chapter 11 where there is a great list of men and women of God and the exploits they have done, men and women of faith. Then in Hebrews 12:1-3: *"Wherefore seeing we also are compassed about with so great a cloud of witnesses, let us lay aside every weight, and the sin which doth so easily beset us, and let us run with patience the race that is set before us, looking unto Jesus the author and finisher of our faith; who for the joy that was set before Him endured the cross, despising the shame, and is set down at the right hand of the throne of God. For consider Him that endured such contradiction of sinners against Himself, lest ye be wearied and faint in your minds."*

The New Living Translation says it this way: *"Therefore, since we are surrounded by such a huge crowd of witnesses to the life of faith, let us strip off every weight that slows us down, especially the sin that so easily trips us up."* First, we need to lay aside anything that is hindering us, lay aside anything that is causing us to stumble. What is that sin in your life? We need to realize what that is. We need to fight the temptation.

Recently a friend, who is a real health nut, said something very profound. She told me she was going through the supermarket and she saw the Krispy Kreme donuts. She said, "Lord, help me." Then she went right on by. This is one of those things I understand but need help doing. I said to her, "You realize what you did? Rather than focusing on the temptation, the donuts, you let them cause you to turn to the source of your help with the temptation. So when you were tempted with that, you immediately said, "Lord, help me." Then you went on.

We need to learn to lay aside that sin, realizing the cost of that sin. Donuts may be just a few calories. But the sin in our lives ... what it cost the Lord Jesus! His blood! His love! We need to fight that temptation and then put it behind us. One translation says we need to remove the obstacles, weights, and excuses and follow God.

A true account is told of a couple in Bakersfield, California. They had never owned a boat, but they had always wanted a boat. They decided if they had a boat, they could enjoy the lake. So they bought a new boat and put it in the water. However, the boat didn't do what they thought it was supposed to do. They couldn't get the boat to go hardly at all, so they puttered up to the marina. They told the man at the marina that they had just bought this brand new boat but it wouldn't do anything. "It just won't go," they said. So the man at the marina checked it out. The motor worked fine. The prop was the right size. They couldn't find anything above the water line that was the problem. One of the other guys at the marina said, "Let me check underneath." He came back up sputtering, almost drowning, because he was laughing under water. The boat was still strapped to the trailer! No one told them they were supposed to unhitch the trailer. They just backed the trailer into the water, putting the whole thing in.

It sounds so ridiculous. But how many of us are trying to live the Christian life, trying to get up to speed, trying to "plane out." It's so smooth. We know that's where we need to be. We've got the right power source. We've got the right tools and equipment. Still we can't do it. It may just be possible that it's the sin that's under the surface that we're still attached to. We need to lay it aside. Get rid of it.

The second thing we need to do: *"Let us run with endurance."* "Endurance" means "patience." It means "don't quit, hang in there." We've all heard it said that the Christian life is not a sprint; it's a marathon. Sometimes it's a cross country marathon. Sometimes it's the high hurdles. We need to run with endurance *"...the race that God has set before us."*

Scriptures teach us that God has a plan for each of our lives. His plan is for us to know His Son, Jesus. He wants to work in us and through us, because He wants to spend eternity with us. Read Paul Billheimer's book, <u>Destined for the Throne.</u> He says that the things we learn in this life will be completed in eternity.

Whatever it is in your life. There may be things in your life that others don't deal with. You have your race. You have your course. You have your things that God has allowed in your life.

He wants us to run patiently, with endurance. Laying aside the things that trip us up; laying aside any excuses we have.

Third, we do this by keeping our eyes on Jesus, the Champion Who initiates and perfects our faith. My dad loved to garden. Then when I married Barbie, my dad and my father-in-law had a real competition. Both of them loved to garden. That must be where I get my love for gardening. And Mossy Mae always gardened also when I was growing up in the 50s and early 60s. People would ask Mossy Mae why she and granddaddy put in such a large garden. She would answer, "Because if the Communists take over, at least we'll have food to eat." She believed that. She canned and practiced that way.

My dad gardened. One day I asked him how he laid off such straight rows. He answered, "Son, the key to layng off straight rows is to pick something at the end of the field and keep your eyes on it." No matter how much you are tempted to look down or to look back and see how straight you've been. If you do that, you'll mess up. As long as you keep your eyes on that focal point, landmark, whatever it is. It can be a clod. It can be a rock or a stick. He said as long as you keep your eyes on that, when you get to the end of the row, then look back. That's how you lay off a straight row.

That lesson so true in the garden is also so real in life. Remember Peter did alright walking on water as long as he kept his eyes on Jesus. But when he looked down and saw the storms around him, he began to sink like a rock. Sometimes if we are not careful, we will want to look back to see how we're doing. When we do, we mess up. Lay aside those sins. Lay aside those obstacles. Lay aside those excuses. "Run with endurance." "Keeping our eyes on Jesus." Keep looking at Him. He's the Champion. Keep our eyes on the end of the line ... eternity! When we get with Him, then we can look around.

Finally, the fourth thing, think of all the hostilities Jesus endured from sinful people. The final thought is to remember Jesus when you want to quit. Think of all He endured. Then you won't become weary and give up. He knows there's going to come a time when you're going to want to give up. Have you ever felt that way? Have you ever thought, "I didn't sign up for this. When I became a Christian, no one told me there would be all this persecution. I'm supposed to have a good attitude and forgive"? All of us at times get weary and think we'll just stay home, pray and read our Bibles.

Right before I got fired from coaching, one of the parents who probably knew something that I didn't know, gave me a book.

The title of the book was <u>It's Hard to Soar with Eagles When You Run With The Buzzards.</u> I remember looking at the title of that book thinking, "I'm soaring with eagles." A few months later, buzzards were all around.

We need to look to Jesus. Lay aside all those weights. Lay aside the obstacles. Lay aside all the excuses. Run with endurance. Keep our eyes on Him. And remember Jesus when we want to quit, when we want to give up.

"Blessed are the pure in heart, for they shall see God." I used to read this and think that the pure in heart are going to see God in Heaven. Now I'm convinced it is far more than that. "Shall see" is a future indicative tense. It means that people with pure hearts will be continually seeing God at work in them and around them. We see His grace. We see His goodness. We see His love. The unconditional love of God. *"Blessed are the pure in heart"* for you will see God working around you all the time. Working in your families. Working in your situations.

In conclusion, this is a true story of Miss Anna Mae Pennica, born blind in 1920. When people lose their sense of hearing or sense of smell or mobility, it is very hard. But to lose your vision!

Anna Mae had never seen. She'd never seen the greens. I love to look at the mountains. Have you noticed the different hues of greens on the mountains? Light green, dark green, green that's almost blue, all these different shades of green. We look around and see God's creation. She had never seen any of that. She was going to a class to learn Braille. She met a man at the class who was also learning Braille but he could see. They fell in love and got married.

For the next 15 years of Anna Mae's life, her husband was her eyes. He would try to explain how a sunset looked. He was her eyes. Then in 1961 a Dr. Thomas Pettit of Jules Stein Eye Institute at UCLA performed surgery on Anna Mae's eyes to correct this rare congenital condition. The surgery was successful and she could see for the first time. She was 62 years old.

She would get up early so she could see the light come in. Things were so much bigger than she had imagined. And so much more brilliant. Her vision was 20/30. She actually passed a driver's exam.

There is a sad part to this story. Dr. Pettit told her this surgery had been available for forty years. For forty years, she had lived in total darkness. If she'd only known!

Apply this to us today: Jesus said, *"Blessed are the pure in heart, for they shall see God."* The technique for curing spiritual blindness has existed for a couple thousand years. The procedure is radical, but it is always 100% effective. When God opens our eyes and gives us a new heart, new eyes to see, He makes us a new creature. We don't have to go around in spiritual darkness any longer. Do you see Him all around you?

"Blessed are the pure in heart, for they shall see God."

BLESSED ARE THE PEACEMAKERS

FOR THEY SHALL BE CALLED THE CHILDREN OF GOD
Matthew 5:9

As Jesus was sharing from the Mount that morning around the Sea of Galilee, it must have been quite a shock to His listeners, especially to this young teacher from Galilee and to the other Jews. I'm sure there were mostly Jews there. How could Jesus ever expect them to overthrow the Roman government and restore Israel back to the days of David and Solomon, when Israel was one of the real powers of the world? How could He expect them to do that by being peacemakers?

I can imagine them shaking their heads saying, "This is crazy." The Roman soldiers aren't going to lay down their weapons because a group of Jews try to overthrow the Roman government and bring Israel back into world prominence. So it made no sense at all to them. Verse nine says: *"Blessed are the peacemakers for they shall be called the children of God."*

Look around us today. Look at the conflict. Look at the turmoil. Look at the terrorist attacks around the world. In light of all this hostility, in light of all the hate, does the calling of verse nine still apply to followers of Christ today to be peacemakers? In a world that is growing more and more hostile to anyone who claims the name of Christ, the world seems bent on destruction and annihilation, is He is still calling us in the midst of all this to be peacemakers? I think the answer is definitely yes.

I want to share with you wisdom from a child: A four-year-old boy had a friend coming over to play one afternoon. It was a rough day for four year olds. They played all right for a while, but then there was a lot of fussing and fighting. The mom had to come in several times to make peace. Finally the mom came in with a snack for a break. She drew her son aside and said, "Son, your friend came over to play with you and you haven't been very nice to him. You need to do a better job of being a good host to him." The little four-year-old boy looked up and said, "Well, Mom, sometimes I'm mean and sometimes I'm not." People are like that, you know.

"Blessed are the peacemakers." As far as I can tell, this is the only time the word Peacemakers is used in the New Testament.

The meaning is illuminated in a verse in James 3:18: *"And the fruit of righteousness is sown in peace of them that make peace."*

It's interesting to me that God called us to be peace*makers* and not peace*keepers*.

If you aren't careful and you try to keep peace, you'll end up like the fellow who had friends in the northern army and friends in the southern army. He wasn't going to take sides, so he wore a blue jacket and gray pants. When they found his body, he'd been shot in both the top and the bottom. Sometimes when you try to keep the peace, you end up being in the middle of something.

Scriptures are clear to us and warn us about a couple of different kinds of people who are not peace makers. First of all, Scriptures warn us about peace *breakers*. Romans 16:17 says: *"Now I make one more appeal, my dear brothers and sisters. Watch out for people who cause divisions and upset people's faith by teaching things contrary to what you have been taught. Stay away from them."*

Verse 18 goes on to say: *"Such people are not serving Christ our Lord. They are serving their own personal interests. By smooth talk and glowing words, they deceive innocent people."*

Notice the writer of this, most likely Paul, was warning them about divisions within the body of Christ, within the church. He cautions them about that. Proverbs 16:27-28 says, *"Scoundrels create trouble; their words are a destructive blaze"* and *"A troublemaker plants seeds of strife; gossip separates the best of friends."*

If we look at this we see that the tongue, like James says, causes all kinds of problems. There is a good section of Scripture that warns us about this in James 3:2-10: *"For in many things we offend all. If any man offend not in word, the same is a perfect man, and able also to bridle the whole body. Behold, we put bits in the horses' mouths that they may obey us; and we turn about their whole body. Behold also the ships, which though they be so great, and are driven of fierce winds, yet are they turned about with a very small helm, wherever the pilot directs them. Even so the tongue is a little member, and boasteth great things. Behold, how great a matter a little fire kindleth! And the tongue is a fire, a world of iniquity; so is the tongue among our members, that it defileth the whole body, and setteth on fire the course of nature; and it is set on fire of hell. For every kind of beasts, and of birds, and of serpents, and of things in the sea, is tamed, and hath been tamed of mankind; but the tongue can no man tame; it is an unruly evil, full of deadly poison. Therewith bless we God, even the Father; and therewith curse we men, which are made after God's image. Out of the same mouth proceedeth blessing and cursing. My brethren, these things ought not to be."*

It shouldn't be this way, peace breakers. And one of the primary tools the enemy uses to break the peace and the fellowship among believers is the tongue. Be careful. We are warned over and over and over. Even be careful if you are framing it in the scope of spirituality. "Let me share something for you to pray about." If that is why it is shared, then take it to the Lord and no one else. No one else. It's hard to "unknow" things once you know them. Some things that are shared should never be shared. Keep it before the Lord. Do not be a peace breaker. He's called us to be a peacemaker. Not a peace keeper. Not a peace breaker.

Now since we've talked so much about peace breakers let me share a little bit about one more category of people we need to be careful about. Peace fakers. I grew up in a home where above all else it was valued: Don't argue. Don't argue. We weren't allowed to argue. It was okay for mom and dad to argue sometimes, but we couldn't argue. So I grew up with peace as the absence of conflict. That's not true. Not true at all.

Bill Hybels, pastor of Willow Creek, shares in one of his books about a friend of his. Over a course of time, he saw this friend take a turn in his personal life and his walk with the Lord that really concerned him. His friend was headed for some turbulent waters unless something changed. Bill was concerned, so he decided he'd invite his friend to lunch and try to talk to him. Over lunch they sat and talked pleasantries and Bill decided it was time to confront his friend.

Bill said, "The reason I asked us to get together is I've seen the direction I think you are headed. You need to know I'm not trying to run your life. I'm very concerned about this direction." And they talked about some things that were going on. The friend got really angry. Bill thought he was going to come across the table. So Bill said, "Okay. Okay. I'm sorry I mentioned it. I'll never mention it again." And he didn't.

Within two years, the friend had ruined his life by the decisions he'd made. Later on Bill ran into him and he said he asked his forgiveness. He said, "I was not a good friend the day I said I'd never mention it again. I should have said 'I'm your friend. I love you. You can hit me if that'll make you feel better, but I'm gonna be in your face until you get this right.'"

But he hadn't. He faked the peace at a great, great cost. I'm convinced that today there are a lot of friendships and a lot of marriages that can die while everything on the outside looks peaceful. But it's not based on truth on the inside. Ephesians 4:24-27: *"That ye put on the new man, which after God is created in righteousness and true holiness. Wherefore putting away lying, speak every man truth with his neighbor; for we are members one of another. Be angry but do not sin; don't let the sun go down on your wrath; neither give place to the devil."*

Don't be a peace faker at the expense of truth. Prayerfully and lovingly speak the truth. My wife always says there is a world of difference between sharing the truth in love and loving to share the truth. Sometimes it makes all the difference in the world of how that's received. Share the truth lovingly after we've taken it to the Lord. Don't wash your brother's feet with a Brillo pad. Wash with tears, softly.

Now I want to talk about what He does call us to do. *"Blessed are the peacemakers for they shall be called the children of God."* So how do I become, or how can I be, a better peacemaker? How do I not be a peace breaker? Not be a peace keeper? And truly not be a peace faker? What does being a peacemaker look like?

The first thing, Romans 5:1 makes it very clear: *"Therefore being justified by faith, we have peace with God through our Lord Jesus Christ."* Ephesians 2:13-14 says: *"But now in Christ Jesus ye who sometimes were far off are made nigh by the blood of Christ. For he is our peace, who hath made both one, and hath broken down the middle wall of partition between us."*

That is the partition between man and God. Jesus Christ did that. He's our peace. You can't be a peace maker until first of all you have experienced the peace that only Jesus Christ can bring. And I want to tell you there's nothing that can take the place of that. If you're angry with God or feel like God's always been angry with you, you need to know that He loves you. You need to know that Jesus died for you. He gave His blood so that He could bring us not only forgiveness for our sins but so that He could bring us peace in that relationship with God. So before you can ever be a peacemaker, you need to know that He is your peace.

So first is being at peace with God. Second is to stop being self-centered. It's not all about you. You say, "I'm not that way." Self-centeredness comes in a lot of different forms. You don't just have to have your own way all the time. Sometimes you just always think people are out to get you.

Just because someone is whispering in the back of the church doesn't mean they are talking about you. Come on. The world doesn't revolve around you. You are not the center of everything. We need to relax. Take a deep breath and step back. Let God be God. We need to enjoy His peace. And we need to love each other with Christ-like love.

He's called us to be peacemakers. It starts with peace with Him. It starts with getting over ourselves. And, thirdly, serving and loving others. Loving and forgiving. Ephesians 4:28-32 says: *"Let him who stole steal no more, but rather let him labor with his hands the thing which is good, that he may have to give to him that needeth."* Make some money so he may have to give to those who have need. *"Let no corrupt communication proceed out of your mouth, but that which is good to the use of edifying, that it may minister grace unto the hearers. And grieve not the Holy Spirit of God, whereby ye are sealed unto the day of redemption. Let all bitterness, and wrath, and anger, and clamour, and evil speaking, be put away from you with all malice. And be ye kind one to another, tenderhearted, forgiving one another, even as God for Christ's sake hath forgiven you."*

We need to walk in that peace that He has given us. We need to know that. He needs to be our peace. We need to get over ourselves and focus on others. We need to be forgiving and kind and loving to each other.

And then, finally, as I was looking at verse nine, I read the commentary of Chuck Smith, pastor of Calvary Chapel, who has gone on to be with the Lord. There is only one thing I took away from his commentary. This suggestion of his jumped off the page at me. "Learn not to speak."

Now let me tell you, I am half woman. My mother was a woman. So I have this woman gene. Not only was my mother a woman, my mother loved to talk. Anyone who knew her knew that she was a talker. I teased her about that, but I miss that talking. If she were here right now, I'd probably still tease her about it. We'd jokingly say this to her but there was a lot of truth in this joking. She and dad started Blairsville Restaurant. For years they ran it and Mom took in the money. We'd jokingly say if someone came into the Blairsville Restaurant and she didn't know them, before they left she would know who they were, where they were from, where they were going, and what they were going to do when they got there. There's a lot of truth to that. That was Mama. She loved to talk.

So I talk. I don't have the skill, but I talk. That's not a skill. And that scares me because Proverbs 10:19 says, *"In the multitude of words, there is no lack of sin"*. I realize that those of us who talk a lot need to throttle it back a little and ask the Lord to put a guard as the Psalmist, David, said, *"Put a guard on my lips"*. Chuck Smith says to be a peacemaker we need to learn not to talk. To listen more. That's me.

So He has called us to be peacemakers. Not peace fakers. Not peace breakers. And surely not peace keepers. He says, *"Blessed are the peacemakers."* There is a sense of contentment. "Oh, how happy!" *"Blessed are the peacemakers."*

Now know this: that even the Prince of Peace, when He came, was misunderstood. He was lied about and ultimately He was crucified. So there are times when even a peacemaker will be persecuted. Look at this again: *"Blessed are the peacemakers, for they shall be called the children of God."*

Someone will say "He looks like his dad," or "She looks just like her mother." I'm convinced that we look the most like our Heavenly Father when we're loving with His love, sharing grace with His grace, and when we are peacemakers.

But look at the end of this: *"...for they shall be called the children of God."*

Who's going to call us "children of God"? The world? I think the world will look and say, "Wow, they're just like Jesus. That's what Jesus would look like. They must be one of His kids." What about our Heavenly Father? I'm convinced that also applies to Him. *"...they shall be called the children of God."*

"That's My son. That's My daughter. That's My boy. That's My girl. Look at them. I love what they're doing when they trust in Me."

"Blessed are the peacemakers; for they shall be called the children of God."

BLESSED ARE THE PERSECUTED

FOR THEIRS IS THE KINGDOM OF HEAVEN
Matthew 5:10

We understand that the Beatitudes are helping us to think and act as Jesus would. This focus is on the last Beatitude, verse ten. Jesus must have known, when He spoke these words, that they were unnatural; that what He was calling us to do is so far beyond ourselves to do. These words *"Blessed are they who are persecuted for righteousness' sake..."* are so important that He emphasized by repeating them again. He even told us to *"Rejoice, and be exceeding glad."*

In reality, we don't even have to be facing persecution, it can just be a bad day, and we have a hard time rejoicing and being exceedingly glad! Jesus understood that and I think that is why He emphasized it. Maybe that's why He saved this for the very last as He transitioned into the heart of His message.

Followers of Jesus understand this; Paul understood this. In Acts 16 we see Paul living this out. He and his traveling companion Silas are in the city of Philippi where they are confronted by a mob that beats them, brings them before the authorities, puts them in chains and throws them in prison. It had been a bad day in Philippi! So we see Paul and Silas in prison, wide awake, not crying the blues or asking God to release them from bondage. No. Scriptures tell us that at midnight they were praying to God and singing praises to God! You know what happens in the rest of that story. It would be several years later, writing from another prison cell, that Paul would write back to the Christians in Philippi with these words in Philippians 4:4: *"Rejoice in the Lord always; and again I say, Rejoice."*

We all know that the longer we live the more opportunities there will be for us to face criticism and opposition. Some will criticize you for what you do and some will criticize you for what you don't do! I want to give us some pointers for persevering in the face of persecution.

The persecution Jesus is speaking about here is clarified in Matthew 5:10 where He says *"...persecuted for righteousness sake."* Again in verse 11, He says *"...for My sake."*

First Peter 4:14 says, *"If ye be reproached for the name of Christ, happy are ye; for the spirit of glory and of God resteth upon you; on their part he is evil spoken of, but on your part he is glorified. But let none of you suffer as a murderer, or as a thief, or as an evildoer, or, as a busybody in other men's matters. Yet if any man suffer as a Christian, let him not be ashamed; but let him glorify God on this behalf."*

If you are persecuted for something you have done, that's not persecution; that's punishment. If the persecution comes because you are a follower of Christ, there is a great reward reserved for you in heaven, but there is a blessing in the process.

Second Timothy 3:12 says this: "Yea, and all that will live godly in Christ Jesus shall suffer persecution." I would rather be called a fool for following God than to have the praises and accolades of men by following the world.

This reminds me of a story told by Franklin Graham. Franklin was going through quite a period of rebellion and his father, Billy Graham, thought Franklin could benefit from spending some time with Sami Dagher. Sami had been a maitre d' at the world famous Phoenicia Hotel in Beirut before the civil war in Lebanon.

Shortly before the war broke out, Sami left the hotel to plant a small church in one of the poorest areas of Lebanon. When he approached the hotel manager to inform him of his resignation, Sami said, "God has called me to preach; I'm leaving the hotel." The reply was, "Leaving! You're a fool! You're crazy! A man in your position making good money and you quit?" Sami said, "I leave for something more important than money; I'm going to preach the name of Jesus Christ." "You're going to give up this position to preach for some god? You must be crazy! I'll tell you the right thing to do. You stay here and make money, Sami; I need you!" Sami said, "No, I can't stay any longer. I've prayed and this is what I must do." The hotel manager really grew angry and shouted, "I curse you! One day, Sami Dagher, you will come to the threshold of my door and you will beg for a crust of bread and I won't give it to you. I will let you starve. You hear my word? Not a crust."

Quite some time later, late at night during some of the heaviest fighting, Sami heard a knock at his door. He told his wife and children to stay where they were and he answered the door. When Sami opened the door, the hotel manager stood there before him. Sami invited him in. "I couldn't sleep," the man said. "I wanted to see how you were doing."

Sami sensed the man had come for another reason but the man wouldn't say. Finally, Sami said, "My friend, it's late. Why have you come to me?" "Oh, nothing, Sami. I just wanted to talk of old times." The man walked to the door and opened it. As he stood in the doorway with his head hung low, he turned to Sami and said, "I have no food. I have not eaten for two days. Do you have anything you could spare?" Sami, of course, gave him something to eat. (Franklin Graham, **Rebel With A Cause**, Thomas Nelson Publishers, 1995, pp164-167)

Today as we talk about the persecution of Christians, we see what's happening around us and we hear of the atrocities of radical Islamist terrorist groups and other groups who are persecuting Christians. We look back at the horrible attack at Columbine High School in Colorado where two young men would ask their classmates if they were a believer in Jesus Christ and if the person said "yes," they would be shot. If they said "no," they let them go.

Recently in one of the terrorist attacks, one of the hostages reported that they were taken to a room and those who could quote correctly from the Quran were given food and comfort.

Those who could not were tortured, killed, and mutilated. The attacks on Christians, even to martyrdom, is so real. People who travel in those areas know first-hand families that have been and continue to be affected by that kind of persecution.

Persecution here in the United States has not risen to that level, but this is what Jesus speaks of when He says, *"Blessed are ye, when men shall revile you, and persecute you, and shall say all manner of evil against you falsely, for my sake."* The word "revile" is not a common word these days, but it appears frequently in the Bible. The word literally means "to make fun of you." So this was used often to describe when people would make fun of, or lie about, or falsely accuse. In John 8:48, Jesus is called a demon-possessed Samaritan. It says, *"Say we not well that thou art a Samaritan, and hast a devil?"* Now that's about as bad a name as they could think of. For a Jew to call someone a Samaritan was bad. So being a demon-possessed Samaritan would be doubly bad.

In John 10:20, they said Jesus *"...hath a devil and is mad..."* In Matthew 27:39-42 it says, *"And they that passed by reviled him, wagging their heads, and saying, Thou that destroyest the temple and buildest it in three days, save thyself. If thou be the Son of God, come down from the cross. Likewise, the Chief priests mocking him, with the scribes and elders, said, He saved others, himself he cannot save. If he be the King of Israel, let him now come down from the cross, and we will believe him."* Peter tells us in chapter 2 verse 23 of his first letter, "Who, when he was *reviled, reviled not again; when he suffered, he threatened not; but committed himself to him that judgeth righteously."* Who is the One that judges righteously? The Lord God Almighty!

Think about that. Jesus was reviled. They accused Him, called Him names, lied about Him, even accused Him of being a drunkard and glutton. I think KJV calls Him a "winebibber." They accused Him because He associated with people of the world. Think about this: Here they are, face to face, **in** His face, with this accusation. Jesus could have looked back at them, into their hearts, named names and accurately named the sins that they were hiding, and He would have been right. When He was reviled, He didn't respond in kind. When He suffered, He didn't threaten. He trusted – "committed himself to" – the Lord God Almighty.

Jesus understood that when they were attacking and accusing Him, when they were lying and demeaning Him, they were attacking His Father.

So when we face similar circumstances there are four things we need to keep in mind. The first is: Consider the Source from which the persecution comes. My dad used to say, "Sometimes you can tell more about a person by who his enemies are than who his friends are." There is a lot of wisdom in that. Ephesians 6:11-12 is a good source for us to keep in mind as we deal with this. It says, "*Put on the whole armor of God, that ye may be able to stand against the wiles of the devil. For we wrestle not against flesh and blood, but against principalities, against powers, against the rulers of the darkness of this world, against spiritual wickedness in high places.*" The writer of Ephesians is reminding us that, as we are confronted with people in our face, people who are angry, they are not the source of the persecution. What we see going on in the world today is fueled by an anger that comes from Satan himself towards God and towards God's people.

If you have walked with the Lord for some time, you know and have probably experienced how you can be attacked spiritually. Satan doesn't go after those "sleeping" people, but those who wake up and start trying to follow God are the ones he wars against. Satan does not fight fair. He will attack you any way he can. And when he can't attack you personally, he goes after your kids, your friends, your family.

Satan will attack anything and anyone you care about because he knows that will hurt you. Satan tried to destroy Jesus before He was ever born. He tried to thwart God's plan from the very foundation of the world in the Garden of Eden. God prepared a sacrifice for Adam and Eve's sin. So an animal gave its life as a foreshadowing of the Lamb of God Who would give His life for us all. The animal skins covered their nakedness as the blood of Jesus Christ would cover our iniquities. And then when Jesus was born, what did Satan try to do? He worked through Herod to kill all baby boys under the age of two, trying again to thwart God's plan. He couldn't attack God so he attacks the Son of God.

The attacks continue on but Jesus marches obediently and sinlessly toward Calvary where He would lay down His life's blood as a payment for our sin. There on a cross and with an empty tomb, Jesus conquered death and hell. So what does Satan do now? He goes after God's children, their families, and the things they love.

In the end times in which we live, as we look for the coming of the Lord, as Christians pray "Come, Lord Jesus!," Evangelicals are burdened to bring as many into the family of God as they can as long as the doors are open.

Recently in Russia, supposedly as an anti-terrorism measure, Putin signed into law making it illegal for churches to share the gospel outside of the church. Until now, our sister church and many other churches in Russia take their message out into the streets, taking the gospel out to where the people are, and God has honored that with a tremendous harvest of souls. Now under this new law, Christians are forbidden to do that. Not only that, but fear is that they will return to the "old days" where Christians were not even allowed to share the gospel with their kids in their own home! The hatred for anything to do with Jesus Christ is only going to intensify. So the words Jesus shared on the mountain that morning are words that are even more applicable to us today. The first thing is to Consider the Source. Know that, when the devil attacks, our warfare is not against the people he uses but a war that must be won in the spiritual realm.

The second thing is: Refuse to Retaliate. Romans 12:17-21 says, *"Recompense to no man evil for evil. Provide things honest in the sight of all men. If it be possible, as much as lieth in you, live peaceably with all men. Dearly beloved, avenge not yourselves, but rather give place unto wrath: for it is written, Vengeance is mine; I will repay, saith the Lord. Therefore, if thine enemy hunger, feed him; if he thirst, give him drink; for in so doing thou shalt heap coals of fire on his head. Be not overcome of evil, but overcome evil with good."*

Jesus modeled that for us. He didn't allow Himself to respond to the accusations, lies, or name-calling. Instead, He was able to trust or commit that to God. Can we do that? When people lie about you,, accuse you falsely, or make fun of you, Consider the Source and Refuse to Retaliate.

The third thing is: Respond as Jesus Would. In Matthew 5:43-45 Jesus says, *"Ye have heard that it hath been said, Thou shalt love thy neighbor and hate thine enemy. But I say unto you, Love your enemies, bless them that curse you, do good to them that hate you, and pray for them which despitefully use you, and persecute you. That ye may be the children of your Father which is in heaven..."* Consider the Source. Refuse to Retaliate. Respond as Jesus Would.

In Matthew 5:12 Jesus says: *"Rejoice and be exceeding glad: for great is your reward in heaven: for so persecuted they the prophets which were before you."* Now we can say that not only were the prophets persecuted but Jesus was also persecuted in the same way.

Second Corinthians 4:16-18 in the New Living Translation says, *"That is why we never give up. Though our bodies are dying, our spirits are being renewed every day. For our present troubles are small and won't last very long. Yet they produce for us a glory that vastly outweighs them and will last forever! So we don't look at the troubles we can see now; rather, we fix our gaze on things that cannot be seen. For the things we see now will soon be gone, but the things we cannot see will last forever."* So the fourth pointer is this: Keep the Reward in Mind "...for great is your reward in heaven..."

Just know, when persecution comes, Jesus knew it would, and He left us some powerful truths to guide us. Consider the Source. Refuse to Retaliate. Respond as Jesus Would. Keep the Reward in Mind.

"Blessed are they which are persecuted for righteousness' sake; for theirs is the kingdom of heaven."

CONCLUSION

YOU ARE THE SALT OF THE EARTH
YOU ARE THE LIGHT OF THE WORLD
Mathew 5:13-16

"Ye are the salt of the earth; but if the salt hath lost its savour, wherewith shall it be salted? It is thenceforth good for nothing, but to be cast out, and to be trodden under foot of men. Ye are the light of the world. A city that is set on an hill cannot be hid. Neither do men light a candle, and put it under a bushel, but on a candlestick; and it giveth light unto all that are in the house. Let your light so shine before men, that they may see your good works, and glorify your Father which is in heaven." Matthew 5:13-16

All of us have heard the stories of someone who finds a painting at a yard sale for $5, and it ends up being a Picasso worth a lot of money. It always amazes me because the original owners never realized the value of what they had in their possession. Or how about an article that sold for $2.48 and was worth almost half a million. That's a pretty good profit.

That's exactly what happened to a man named Michael Sparks. Stan Cathy was engaged to be married. He thought before the wedding day he needed to do some cleaning out.

He was cleaning out his garage, donating a lot of stuff to Goodwill. He noticed an old document that had been hanging on his wall for over ten years, so he threw it in the Goodwill pile. Michael Sparks saw this document at the Goodwill store. It was a very rare 1823 copy of the Declaration of Independence. He bought it for $2.48. Later he sold it at an auction for almost half a million dollars.

Now I don't mind when my wife Barbie and her friend Evelyn want to look for a Goodwill store. I'm just looking for old documents. Barbie and I have the old California raisin mugs. We also have a complete set of Flintstone mugs we got from Dairy Queen. We're just waiting for the market to demand these. We also have two shelves of Avon bottles in a display cabinet. They're classic. One day...

Barbie and I have invested in these for our children and grandchildren. The sad thing is that our two children, Zach and Paige, say when the Lord calls us home, these will be the first things to go into a yard sale. So if you hear that the

Lord calls Barbie and me home soon; and you hear there is a yard sale on EZ Street, you need to get there quickly. Paige and Zach do not know the value of these things.

You are of great value to our God. Sometimes we don't feel that valuable. Maybe you feel like you failed God in something He has called you to do. You may feel of no value. You may feel you failed Him horribly in your marriage. In your second marriage. Your third marriage. You tell Him, "Lord, I have messed up so many times. You can't value me." Maybe you feel like you failed Him with your kids. When your kids were little, you weren't in the place with the Lord that you are now. Your life was just consumed with providing. You poured all your time into your career to provide for them. Now your kids are grown and gone and you realize you didn't invest in them like you wish you had. You didn't have time for them, and now they don't have time for you. You feel like a failure because of all your mistakes. I can see why He'd value other people, but does He really love ME?

When it comes to life, sometimes we feel like we're just going through the motions. Satan, our enemy, is quick to fan the flame of that stinkin' thinkin'. He tells you God doesn't love you. He tells you that you're no good, no good to God. But God's Word tells us something completely different.

God's Word tells us that God loves us no matter what. No matter what we've done, no matter how bad we've messed it up, we can't stop Him from loving us. He IS love! That amazes me. That humbles me. He loves you! You are of great value to Him!

He wants us to live our lives out in the reality of who we are in Him. These verses in Matthew 5 say *"You ARE the salt of the earth ... You ARE the light of the world."* I always focus on what I need to DO. I need to get right. Jesus says this is who you ARE.

Remember the context of this: Jesus sees the multitudes and He goes up onto a mountain. His disciples have come there and He is teaching them. I'm convinced this is no coincidence, that Jesus does everything perfectly. Jesus has never said, "Oops! I didn't see that coming. I messed up there, didn't I Father?" Jesus, all-knowing God, does everything in the right time and in the right way. So, He has gone through these Beatitudes: the poor in spirit, the mourning and grieving, the meek, the gentle, the tender, those who hunger and thirst after righteousness, the merciful, those who are pure in heart, the peacemakers, those who are persecuted.

He has listed these character qualities of who we are. Now in these verses, Jesus gives us a job description. He not only loves us; He not only values us; He has a job for each of us who are followers of His.

Here are the broad boundaries of His job description for us. He wants us to live out who we are in Him. We are where He has placed us. *"You are the salt of the earth ...... You are the light of the world. "*

At camp one year, the theme was "Set Apart." God has called us as His children. He set us apart. So at camp, they decided to begin each day with a skit. Then all day long the classes and the lessons would be built on that skit. The skits were all centered around Jesus calling Peter and the disciples to follow Him. Just like He calls us, "Come and follow Me."

Tuesday morning the kids all go down to the lake. There are two boats out there with different counselors in full wardrobe. They are out fishing, cleaning the nets. They've been fishing all night and caught nothing. The kids are up on the bank watching. Then another counselor comes portraying Jesus. He walks down the hill, through the kids, talking to them.

He goes down to the dock and calls out to Peter, "Hey, Peter, can I get into your boat and go out and talk to these people?" He gets in the boat and says a few words to the kids. Then he turns to Peter and asks if he'd caught anything. Peter tells him they'd fished all night and caught nothing. He tells then to throw their nets into the water on the right side of the boat. They do and pull it out with a net full of fish! The other guys needed to come over and help them get to the shore. When they get to the shore, they are amazed. Then Jesus says to Peter, "Come and follow Me." He says to the disciples, "Come and follow Me."

This is a very familiar story. During the first week of camp, teen week, as Jesus walks off into the woods, Peter follows Him. I hear a rumble from the kids, "What about the fish?" "What about the boat?" That's me! I'd be, "Jesus, You gave us all these fish. I gotta take 'em home and clean 'em. Where can I meet You tomorrow?"

Wednesday morning they go to the pool. That's where Peter is walking on water. There is a storm. Jesus bids Peter to walk to Him. And He does .... As long as he keeps his eyes on Jesus.

The skit Thursday morning is back at the lake. After Jesus' crucifixion and resurrection, the disciples are fishing again. Haven't caught anything again. (The moral of the story is if you go fishing, go fishing with Jesus if you want to catch any fish.) Jesus is cooking fish on the shore. He tells them again, "Throw your nets on the right side." They realize it's Jesus. That's when Jesus says to Peter, *"Do you love Me? ..... Then feed My sheep."*

During elementary week, they did this skit. Then Jesus walks off into the woods and Peter follows Him. One of the young campers runs up and grabs hold of Jesus and says, "Jesus, I need to be saved."

So right then and there, two counselors led this young boy to faith in Jesus Christ. That's exactly what Jesus would do. And it could happen to you. "

Therefore, if anyone (any man or woman, boy or girl) *is in Christ, they are a new creation; old things have passed away; behold, all things are new."* 2 Corinthians 5:17

If you've never trusted Him as your Savior, it starts with being born again. But that's not the landing strip; that's the launching pad.

You are of great value to Him! He's got a job description for you. Take some time to think about it.

In conclusion, let's take another look at these Beatitudes:

Blessed are the poor in spirit: for theirs is the kingdom of heaven.
Blessed are they that mourn: for they shall be comforted.
Blessed are the meek: for they shall inherit the earth.
Blessed are they which do hunger and thirst after righteousness: for they shall be filled.
Blessed are the merciful: for they shall obtain mercy.
Blessed are the pure in heart: for they shall see God.
Blessed are the peacemakers: for they shall be called the children of God.
Blessed are they which are persecuted for righteousness' sake: for theirs is the kingdom of heaven."

Matthew 5:1-10

79394577R00072

Made in the USA
Lexington, KY
20 January 2018